DATE DUE			
JAN 2 6 1987			
DEC 0 5 2001			

War and Moral Responsibility

War and Moral Responsibility

A *Philosophy & Public Affairs* Reader

Edited by MARSHALL COHEN, THOMAS NAGEL, and THOMAS SCANLON

Contributors

R. B. BRANDT

R. M. HARE

SANFORD LEVINSON

DAVID MALAMENT

THOMAS NAGEL

MICHAEL WALZER

RICHARD WASSERSTROM

Princeton University Press
Princeton, New Jersey

ALL RIGHTS RESERVED
L.C. Card: 73-8267
ISBN 0-691-01980-0 (paperback edn.)
ISBN 0-691-07198-5 (hardcover edn.)

The essays in this book originally appeared
in the quarterly journal *Philosophy &
Public Affairs*, published by Princeton
University Press.

Michael Walzer, "World War II: Why
Was This War Different?" *P&PA* 1, no. 1
(Fall 1971): copyright © 1971 by Prince-
ton University Press. Thomas Nagel,
"War and Massacre," *P&PA* 1, no. 2
(Winter 1972); R. B. Brandt, "Utilitarian-
ism and the Rules of War," *P&PA* 1, no.
2 (Winter 1972); David Malament,
"Selective Conscientious Objection and
the *Gillette* Decision," *P&PA* 1, no. 4
(Summer 1972): copyright © 1972 by
Princeton University Press. Michael
Walzer, "Political Action: The Problem
of Dirty Hands," *P&PA* 2, no. 2 (Winter
1973); Sanford Levinson, "Responsibility
for Crimes of War," *P&PA* 2, no. 3
(Spring 1973): copyright © 1973 by
Princeton University Press. R. M. Hare,
"Rules of War and Moral Reasoning,"
P&PA 1, no. 2 (Winter 1972): copyright
© 1972 by R. M. Hare.

First Princeton Paperback Printing, 1974
First Hardcover Printing, 1974

Printed in the United States of America
by Princeton University Press,
Princeton, New Jersey

CONTENTS

PREFACE

Philosophy & Public Affairs was founded in the belief that issues of public concern often have a philosophical dimension and that a philosophical examination of these issues can contribute to their clarification and to their resolution. The editors believe that this expectation is borne out by the following essays, drawn from the first two volumes of *Philosophy & Public Affairs*, and written by lawyers and political scientists as well as by philosophers. Part I of this volume contains a symposium on the conduct of war, which examines the ethical and legal sources of restrictions on military methods and aims. The symposiasts, Thomas Nagel, Richard B. Brandt, and R. M. Hare, relate the details of their discussion to the most general and fundamental considerations of moral theory. Here the traditional theoretical controversy between utilitarianism and anti-utilitarianism is shown to have important practical consequences. This debate in turn is the subject of Michael Walzer's essay on the dilemmas of moral action and the problem of "dirty hands" in politics.

The essays in Part II focus on problems arising out of World War II and the Vietnam war. Here Michael Walzer discusses the unique character of Nazism and asks whether ultimate evil of this sort does not permit those who oppose it to set aside the normal prohibitions on military conduct. Sanford Levinson examines the Nuremberg trials and, in particular, their attempt to establish canons of responsibility within the elaborate bureaucratic organizations that govern modern nations and their military forces. Richard Wasserstrom challenges some widespread assumptions about the significance, and especially the legal significance, of the Nuremberg trials for those who have moral objections to military service in a war they regard as morally illegitimate. Finally, David Malament criticizes the Supreme Court's decision in the *Gillette* case, arguing that the draft law is unconstitutional because it does not permit selective conscientious objection. The moral problems addressed by the essays in this collection are given special immediacy by events of the recent past, but those problems continue to face us. The freedom, and indeed, the lives of countless persons depend on the answers given to the questions addressed in these important essays. M.C., T.N., T.S.

War and Moral Responsibility

PART I

THOMAS NAGEL   War and Massacre[1]

From the apathetic reaction to atrocities committed in Vietnam by
the United States and its allies, one may conclude that moral restrictions on the conduct of war command almost as little sympathy
among the general public as they do among those charged with the
formation of U.S. military policy. Even when restrictions on the conduct of warfare are defended, it is usually on legal grounds alone:
their moral basis is often poorly understood. I wish to argue that
certain restrictions are neither arbitrary nor merely conventional,
and that their validity does not depend simply on their usefulness.
There is, in other words, a moral basis for the rules of war, even
though the conventions now officially in force are far from giving it
perfect expression.

I

   No elaborate moral theory is required to account for what is wrong
in cases like the Mylai massacre, since it did not serve, and was not
intended to serve, any strategic purpose. Moreover, if the participation of the United States in the Indo-Chinese war is entirely wrong
to begin with, then that engagement is incapable of providing a
justification for *any* measures taken in its pursuit—not only for the
measures which are atrocities in every war, however just its aims.
   But this war has revealed attitudes of a more general kind, that
influenced the conduct of earlier wars as well. After it has ended, we

   1. This paper grew out of discussions at the Society for Ethical and Legal
Philosophy, and I am indebted to my fellow members for their help.

shall still be faced with the problem of how warfare may be conducted, and the attitudes that have resulted in the specific conduct
of this war will not have disappeared. Moreover, similar problems
can arise in wars or rebellions fought for very different reasons, and
against very different opponents. It is not easy to keep a firm grip
on the idea of what is not permissible in warfare, because while
some military actions are obvious atrocities, other cases are more
difficult to assess, and the general principles underlying these judgments remain obscure. Such obscurity can lead to the abandonment
of sound intuitions in favor of criteria whose rationale may be more
obvious. If such a tendency is to be resisted, it will require a better
understanding of the restrictions than we now have.

I propose to discuss the most general moral problem raised by
the conduct of warfare: the problem of means and ends. In one view,
there are limits on what may be done even in the service of an end
worth pursuing—and even when adherence to the restriction may be
very costly. A person who acknowledges the force of such restrictions
can find himself in acute moral dilemmas. He may believe, for example, that by torturing a prisoner he can obtain information necessary to prevent a disaster, or that by obliterating one village with
bombs he can halt a campaign of terrorism. If he believes that the
gains from a certain measure will clearly outweigh its costs, yet
still suspects that he ought not to adopt it, then he is in a dilemma
produced by the conflict between two disparate categories of moral
reason: categories that may be called *utilitarian* and *absolutist*.

Utilitarianism gives primacy to a concern with what will *happen*.
Absolutism gives primacy to a concern with what one is *doing*. The
conflict between them arises because the alternatives we face are
rarely just choices between *total outcomes*: they are also choices between alternative pathways or measures to be taken. When one of
the choices is to do terrible things to another person, the problem
is altered fundamentally; it is no longer merely a question of which
outcome would be worse.

Few of us are completely immune to either of these types of moral
intuition, though in some people, either naturally or for doctrinal
reasons, one type will be dominant and the other suppressed or weak.
But it is perfectly possible to feel the force of both types of reason

very strongly; in that case the moral dilemma in certain situations of crisis will be acute, and it may appear that every possible course of action or inaction is unacceptable for one reason or another.

II

Although it is this dilemma that I propose to explore, most of the discussion will be devoted to its absolutist component. The utilitarian component is straightforward by comparison, and has a natural appeal to anyone who is not a complete skeptic about ethics. Utilitarianism says that one should try, either individually or through institutions, to maximize good and minimize evil (the definition of these categories need not enter into the schematic formulation of the view), and that if faced with the possibility of preventing a great evil by producing a lesser, one should choose the lesser evil. There are certainly problems about the formulation of utilitarianism, and much has been written about it, but its intent is morally transparent. Nevertheless, despite the addition of various refinements, it continues to leave large portions of ethics unaccounted for. I do not suggest that some form of absolutism can account for them all, only that an examination of absolutism will lead us to see the complexity, and perhaps the incoherence, of our moral ideas.

Utilitarianism certainly justifies *some* restrictions on the conduct of warfare. There are strong utilitarian reasons for adhering to any limitation which seems natural to most people—particularly if the limitation is widely accepted already. An exceptional measure which seems to be justified by its results in a particular conflict may create a precedent with disastrous long-term effects.[2] It may even be argued that war involves violence on such a scale that it is never justified on utilitarian grounds—the consequences of refusing to go to war will never be as bad as the war itself would be, even if atrocities were not committed. Or in a more sophisticated vein it might be claimed that a uniform policy of never resorting to military force would do less harm in the long run, if followed consistently, than a policy of deciding each case on utilitarian grounds (even though on occasion

2. Straightforward considerations of national interest often tend in the same direction: the inadvisability of using nuclear weapons seems to be overdetermined in this way.

particular applications of the pacifist policy might have worse results than a specific utilitarian decision). But I shall not consider these arguments, for my concern is with reasons of a different kind, which may remain when reasons of utility and interest fail.[3]

In the final analysis, I believe that the dilemma cannot always be resolved. While not every conflict between absolutism and utilitarianism creates an insoluble dilemma, and while it is certainly right to adhere to absolutist restrictions unless the utilitarian considerations favoring violation are overpoweringly weighty and extremely certain —nevertheless, when that special condition is met, it may become impossible to adhere to an absolutist position. What I shall offer, therefore, is a somewhat qualified defense of absolutism. I believe it underlies a valid and fundamental type of moral judgment—which cannot be reduced to or overridden by other principles. And while there may be other principles just as fundamental, it is particularly important not to lose confidence in our absolutist intuitions, for they are often the only barrier before the abyss of utilitarian apologetics for large-scale murder.

III

One absolutist position that creates no problems of interpretation is pacifism: the view that one may not kill another person under any circumstances, no matter what good would be achieved or evil averted thereby. The type of absolutist position that I am going to discuss is different. Pacifism draws the conflict with utilitarian considerations very starkly. But there are other views according to which violence may be undertaken, even on a large scale, in a clearly just cause, so long as certain absolute restrictions on the character and direction of that violence are observed. The line is drawn somewhat closer to the bone, but it exists.

The philosopher who has done most to advance contemporary philosophical discussion of such a view, and to explain it to those

3. These reasons, moreover, have special importance in that they are available even to one who denies the appropriateness of utilitarian considerations in international matters. He may acknowledge limitations on what may be done to the soldiers and civilians of other countries in pursuit of his nation's military objectives, while denying that one country should in general consider the interests of nationals of other countries in determining its policies.

unfamiliar with its extensive treatment in Roman Catholic moral
theology, is G.E.M. Anscombe. In 1958 Miss Anscombe published a
pamphlet entitled *Mr. Truman's Degree*,[4] on the occasion of the
award by Oxford University of an honorary doctorate to Harry
Truman. The pamphlet explained why she had opposed the decision
to award that degree, recounted the story of her unsuccessful opposition, and offered some reflections on the history of Truman's decision
to drop atom bombs on Hiroshima and Nagasaki, and on the difference between murder and allowable killing in warfare. She pointed
out that the policy of deliberately killing large numbers of civilians
either as a means or as an end in itself did not originate with Truman, and was common practice among all parties during World
War II for some time before Hiroshima. The Allied area bombings
of German cities by conventional explosives included raids which
killed more civilians than did the atomic attacks; the same is true of
certain fire-bomb raids on Japan.

The policy of attacking the civilian population in order to induce
an enemy to surrender, or to damage his morale, seems to have been
widely accepted in the civilized world, and seems to be accepted
still, at least if the stakes are high enough. It gives evidence of a
moral conviction that the deliberate killing of noncombatants—wom-
en, children, old people—is permissible if enough can be gained by it.
This follows from the more general position that any means can in
principle be justified if it leads to a sufficiently worthy end. Such an
attitude is evident not only in the more spectacular current weapons
systems but also in the day-to-day conduct of the nonglobal war in
Indochina: the indiscriminate destructiveness of antipersonnel weapons, napalm, and aerial bombardment; cruelty to prisoners; massive
relocation of civilians; destruction of crops; and so forth. An abso-

4. (Privately printed.) See also her essay "War and Murder," in *Nuclear
Weapons and Christian Conscience*, ed. Walter Stein (London, 1963). The
present paper is much indebted to these two essays throughout. These and
related subjects are extensively treated by Paul Ramsey in *The Just War* (New
York, 1968). Among recent writings that bear on the moral problem are
Jonathan Bennett, "Whatever the Consequences," *Analysis* 26, no. 3 (1966):
83-102; and Philippa Foot, "The Problem of Abortion and the Doctrine of the
Double Effect," *The Oxford Review* 5 (1967): 5-15. Miss Anscombe's replies
are "A Note on Mr. Bennett," *Analysis* 26, no. 3 (1966): 208, and "Who is
Wronged?" *The Oxford Review* 5 (1967): 16-17.

lutist position opposes to this the view that certain acts cannot be justified no matter what the consequences. Among those acts is murder—the deliberate killing of the harmless: civilians, prisoners of war, and medical personnel.

In the present war such measures are sometimes said to be regrettable, but they are generally defended by reference to military necessity and the importance of the long-term consequences of success or failure in the war. I shall pass over the inadequacy of this consequentialist defense in its own terms. (That is the dominant form of moral criticism of the war, for it is part of what people mean when they ask, "Is it worth it?") I am concerned rather to account for the inappropriateness of offering any defense of that kind for such actions.

Many people feel, without being able to say much more about it, that something has gone seriously wrong when certain measures are admitted into consideration in the first place. The fundamental mistake is made there, rather than at the point where the overall benefit of some monstrous measure is judged to outweigh its disadvantages, and it is adopted. An account of absolutism might help us to understand this. If it is not allowable to *do* certain things, such as killing unarmed prisoners or civilians, then no argument about what will happen if one doesn't do them can show that doing them would be all right.

Absolutism does not, of course, require one to ignore the consequences of one's acts. It operates as a limitation on utilitarian reasoning, not as a substitute for it. An absolutist can be expected to try to maximize good and minimize evil, so long as this does not require him to transgress an absolute prohibition like that against murder. But when such a conflict occurs, the prohibition takes complete precedence over any consideration of consequences. Some of the results of this view are clear enough. It requires us to forgo certain potentially useful military measures, such as the slaughter of hostages and prisoners or indiscriminate attempts to reduce the enemy civilian population by starvation, epidemic infectious diseases like anthrax and bubonic plague, or mass incineration. It means that we cannot deliberate on whether such measures are justified by the fact that they will avert still greater evils, for as intentional measures they cannot be justified in terms of any consequences whatever.

Someone unfamiliar with the events of this century might imagine that utilitarian arguments, or arguments of national interest, would suffice to deter measures of this sort. But it has become evident that such considerations are insufficient to prevent the adoption and employment of enormous antipopulation weapons once their use is considered a serious moral possibility. The same is true of the piecemeal wiping out of rural civilian populations in airborne antiguerrilla warfare. Once the door is opened to calculations of utility and national interest, the usual speculations about the future of freedom, peace, and economic prosperity can be brought to bear to ease the consciences of those responsible for a certain number of charred babies.

For this reason alone it is important to decide what is wrong with the frame of mind which allows such arguments to begin. But it is also important to understand absolutism in the cases where it genuinely conflicts with utility. Despite its appeal, it is a paradoxical position, for it can require that one refrain from choosing the lesser of two evils when that is the only choice one has. And it is additionally paradoxical because, unlike pacifism, it permits one to do horrible things to people in some circumstances but not in others.

IV

Before going on to say what, if anything, lies behind the position, there remain a few relatively technical matters which are best discussed at this point.

First, it is important to specify as clearly as possible the kind of thing to which absolutist prohibitions can apply. We must take seriously the proviso that they concern what we deliberately do to people. There could not, for example, without incoherence, be an absolute prohibition against *bringing about* the death of an innocent person. For one may find oneself in a situation in which, no matter what one does, some innocent people will die as a result. I do not mean just that there are cases in which someone will die no matter what one does, because one is not in a position to affect the outcome one way or the other. That, it is to be hoped, is one's relation to the deaths of most innocent people. I have in mind, rather, a case in which someone is bound to die, but who it is will depend on what one does. Sometimes these situations have natural causes, as when too few resources (medicine, lifeboats) are available to rescue everyone threatened with a certain catastrophe. Sometimes the situations are man-made, as when the only way to control a campaign of terrorism is to employ terrorist tactics against the community from which it has arisen. Whatever one does in cases such as these, some innocent people will die as a result. If the absolutist prohibition forbade doing what would result in the deaths of innocent people, it would have the consequence that in such cases nothing one could do would be morally permissible.

This problem is avoided, however, because what absolutism forbids is *doing* certain things to people, rather than bringing about certain *results*. Not everything that happens to others as a result of what one does is something that one has *done* to them. Catholic moral theology seeks to make this distinction precise in a doctrine known as the law of double effect, which asserts that there is a morally relevant distinction between bringing about the death of an innocent person deliberately, either as an end in itself or as a means, and bringing it about as a side effect of something else one does deliberately. In the latter case, even if the outcome is foreseen, it is not murder, and does not fall under the absolute prohibition, though of course it may still be wrong for other reasons (reasons of utility, for example). Briefly, the principle states that one is sometimes permitted knowingly to bring about as a side effect of one's actions something which it would be absolutely impermissible to bring about deliberately as an end or as a means. In application to war or revolution, the law of double effect permits a certain amount of civilian carnage as a side effect of bombing munitions plants or attacking enemy soldiers. And even this is permissible only if the cost is not too great to be justified by one's objectives.

However, despite its importance and its usefulness in accounting for certain plausible moral judgments, I do not believe that the law of double effect is a generally applicable test for the consequences of an absolutist position. Its own application is not always clear, so that it introduces uncertainty where there need not be uncertainty.

In Indochina, for example, there is a great deal of aerial bombardment, strafing, spraying of napalm, and employment of pellet- or needle-spraying antipersonnel weapons against rural villages in which guerrillas are suspected to be hiding, or from which small-arms fire has been received. The majority of those killed and wounded in these aerial attacks are reported to be women and children, even when some combatants are caught as well. However, the government regards these civilian casualties as a regrettable side effect of what is a legitimate attack against an armed enemy.

It might be thought easy to dismiss this as sophistry: if one bombs, burns, or strafes a village containing a hundred people, twenty of whom one believes to be guerrillas, so that by killing most of them one will be statistically likely to kill most of the guerrillas, then isn't one's attack on the group of one hundred a *means* of destroying the guerrillas, pure and simple? If one makes no attempt to discriminate between guerrillas and civilians, as is impossible in a aerial attack on a small village, then one cannot regard as a mere side effect the deaths of those in the group that one would not have bothered to kill if more selective means had been available.

The difficulty is that this argument depends on one particular description of the act, and the reply might be that the means used against the guerrillas is not: killing everybody in the village—but rather: obliteration bombing of the *area* in which the twenty guerrillas are known to be located. If there are civilians in the area as well, they will be killed as a side effect of such action.[5]

Because of casuistical problems like this, I prefer to stay with the original, unanalyzed distinction between what one does to people and what merely happens to them as a result of what one does. The law of double effect provides an approximation to that distinction in many cases, and perhaps it can be sharpened to the point where it does better than that. Certainly the original distinction itself needs clarification, particularly since some of the things we do to people involve things happening to them as a result of other things we do. In a case like the one discussed, however, it is clear that by bombing the village one slaughters and maims the civilians in it. Whereas by giving the only available medicine to one of two sufferers from a disease, one does not kill the other, even if he dies as a result.

The second technical point to take up concerns a possible misinterpretation of this feature of the position. The absolutist focus on actions rather than outcomes does not merely introduce a new, out-

5. This counterargument was suggested by Rogers Albritton.

standing item into the catalogue of evils. That is, it does not say that the worst thing in the world is the deliberate murder of an innocent person. For if that were all, then one could presumably justify one such murder on the ground that it would prevent several others, or ten thousand on the ground that they would prevent a hundred thousand more. That is a familiar argument. But if this is allowable, then there is no absolute prohibition against murder after all. Absolutism requires that we *avoid* murder at all costs, not that we *prevent* it at all costs.[6]

Finally, let me remark on a frequent criticism of absolutism that depends on a misunderstanding. It is sometimes suggested that such prohibitions depend on a kind of moral self-interest, a primary obligation to preserve one's own moral purity, to keep one's hands clean no matter what happens to the rest of the world. If this were the position, it might be exposed to the charge of self-indulgence. After all, what gives one man a right to put the purity of his soul or the cleanness of his hands above the lives or welfare of large numbers of other people? It might be argued that a public servant like Truman has no right to put himself first in that way; therefore if he is convinced that the alternatives would be worse, he must give the order to drop the bombs, and take the burden of those deaths on himself, as he must do other distasteful things for the general good.

But there are two confusions behind the view that moral self-interest underlies moral absolutism. First, it is a confusion to suggest that the need to preserve one's moral purity might be the *source* of an obligation. For if by committing murder one sacrifices one's moral purity or integrity, that can only be because there is *already* something wrong with murder. The general reason against committing murder cannot therefore be merely that it makes one an immoral person. Secondly, the notion that one might sacrifice one's moral integrity justifiably, in the service of a sufficiently worthy end, is an incoherent notion. For if one were justified in making such a sacrifice (or even morally required to make it), then one would not be

6. Someone might of course acknowledge the *moral relevance* of the distinction between deliberate and nondeliberate killing, without being an absolutist. That is, he might believe simply that it was *worse* to bring about a death deliberately than as a secondary effect. But that would be merely a special assignment of value, and not an absolute prohibition.

sacrificing one's moral integrity by adopting that course: one would be preserving it.

Moral absolutism is not unique among moral theories in requiring each person to do what will preserve his own moral purity in all circumstances. This is equally true of utilitarianism, or of any other theory which distinguishes between right and wrong. Any theory which defines the right course of action in various circumstances and asserts that one should adopt that course, ipso facto asserts that one should do what will preserve one's moral purity, simply because the right course of action *is* what will preserve one's moral purity in those circumstances. Of course utilitarianism does not assert that this is *why* one should adopt that course, but we have seen that the same is true of absolutism.

v

It is easier to dispose of false explanations of absolutism than to produce a true one. A positive account of the matter must begin with the observation that war, conflict, and aggression are relations between persons. The view that it can be wrong to consider merely the overall effect of one's actions on the general welfare comes into prominence when those actions involve relations with others. A man's acts usually affect more people than he deals with directly, and those effects must naturally be considered in his decisions. But if there are special principles governing the manner in which he should *treat* people, that will require special attention to the particular persons toward whom the act is directed, rather than just to its total effect.

Absolutist restrictions in warfare appear to be of two types: restrictions on the class of persons at whom aggression or violence may be directed and restrictions on the manner of attack, given that the object falls within that class. These can be combined, however, under the principle that hostile treatment of any person must be justified in terms of something *about that person* which makes the treatment appropriate. Hostility is a personal relation, and it must be suited to its target. One consequence of this condition will be that certain persons may not be subjected to hostile treatment in war at all, since nothing about them justifies such treatment. Others will be proper objects of hostility only in certain circumstances, or when they are engaged in certain pursuits. And the appropriate manner and extent of hostile treatment will depend on what is justified by the particular case.

A coherent view of this type will hold that extremely hostile behavior toward another is compatible with treating him as a person—even perhaps as an end in himself. This is possible only if one has not automatically stopped treating him as a person as soon as one starts to fight with him. If hostile, aggressive, or combative treatment of others always violated the condition that they be treated as human beings, it would be difficult to make further distinctions on that score *within* the class of hostile actions. That point of view, on the level of international relations, leads to the position that if complete pacifism is not accepted, no holds need be barred at all, and we may slaughter and massacre to our hearts' content, if it seems advisable. Such a position is often expressed in discussions of war crimes.

But the fact is that ordinary people do not believe this about conflicts, physical or otherwise, between individuals, and there is no more reason why it should be true of conflicts between nations. There seems to be a perfectly natural conception of the distinction between fighting clean and fighting dirty. To fight dirty is to direct one's hostility or aggression not at its proper object, but at a peripheral target which may be more vulnerable, and through which the proper object can be attacked indirectly. This applies in a fist fight, an election campaign, a duel, or a philosophical argument. If the concept is general enough to apply to all these matters, it should apply to war—both to the conduct of individual soldiers and to the conduct of nations.

Suppose that you are a candidate for public office, convinced that the election of your opponent would be a disaster, that he is an unscrupulous demagogue who will serve a narrow range of interests and seriously infringe the rights of those who disagree with him; and suppose you are convinced that you cannot defeat him by conventional means. Now imagine that various unconventional means present themselves as possibilities: you possess information about his sex life which would scandalize the electorate if made public; or you learn that his wife is an alcoholic or that in his youth he was associated for a brief period with a proscribed political party, and you believe that this information could be used to blackmail him into withdrawing his candidacy; or you can have a team of your supporters flatten the tires of a crucial subset of his supporters on election day; or you are in a position to stuff the ballot boxes; or, more simply, you can have him assassinated. What is wrong with these methods, given that they will achieve an overwhelmingly desirable result?

There are, of course, many things wrong with them: some are against the law; some infringe the procedures of an electoral process to which you are presumably committed by taking part in it; very importantly, some may backfire, and it is in the interest of all political candidates to adhere to an unspoken agreement not to allow certain personal matters to intrude into a campaign. But that is not all. We have in addition the feeling that these measures, these methods of attack are *irrelevant* to the issue between you and your opponent, that in taking them up you would not be directing yourself to that which makes him an object of your opposition. You would be directing your attack not at the true target of your hostility, but at peripheral targets that happen to be vulnerable.

The same is true of a fight or argument outside the framework of any system of regulations or law. In an altercation with a taxi driver over an excessive fare, it is inappropriate to taunt him about his accent, flatten one of his tires, or smear chewing gum on his windshield; and it remains inappropriate even if he casts aspersions on your race, politics, or religion, or dumps the contents of your suitcase into the street.[7]

The importance of such restrictions may vary with the seriousness of the case; and what is unjustifiable in one case may be justified in a more extreme one. But they all derive from a single principle: that hostility or aggression should be directed at its true object. This means both that it should be directed at the person or persons who provoke it and that it should aim more specifically at what is provocative about them. The second condition will determine what form the hostility may appropriately take.

7. Why, on the other hand, does it seem appropriate, rather than irrelevant, to punch someone in the mouth if he insults you? The answer is that in our culture it is an insult to punch someone in the mouth, and not just an injury. This reveals, by the way, a perfectly unobjectionable sense in which convention may play a part in determining exactly what falls under an absolutist restriction and what does not. I am indebted to Robert Fogelin for this point.

It is evident that some idea of the relation in which one should stand to other people underlies this principle, but the idea is difficult to state. I believe it is roughly this: whatever one does to another person intentionally must be aimed at him as a subject, with the intention that he receive it as a subject. It should manifest an attitude to *him* rather than just to the situation, and he should be able to recognize it and identify himself as its object. The procedures by which such an attitude is manifested need not be addressed to the person directly. Surgery, for example, is not a form of personal confrontation but part of a medical treatment that can be offered to a patient face to face and received by him as a response to his needs and the natural outcome of an attitude toward *him*.

Hostile treatment, unlike surgery, is already addressed *to* a person, and does not take its interpersonal meaning from a wider context. But hostile acts can serve as the expression or implementation of only a limited range of attitudes to the person who is attacked. Those attitudes in turn have as objects certain real or presumed characteristics or activities of the person which are thought to justify them. When this background is absent, hostile or aggressive behavior can no longer be intended for the reception of the victim as a subject. Instead it takes on the character of a purely bureaucratic operation. This occurs when one attacks someone who is not the true object of one's hostility—the true object may be someone else, who can be attacked through the victim; or one may not be manifesting a hostile attitude toward anyone, but merely using the easiest available path to some desired goal. One finds oneself not facing or addressing the victim at all, but operating on him—without the larger context of personal interaction that surrounds a surgical operation.

If absolutism is to defend its claim to priority over considerations of utility, it must hold that the maintenance of a direct interpersonal response to the people one deals with is a requirement which no advantages can justify one in abandoning. The requirement is absolute only if it rules out any calculation of what would justify its violation. I have said earlier that there may be circumstances so extreme that they render an absolutist position untenable. One may find then that one has no choice but to do something terrible. Nevertheless, even in such cases absolutism retains its force in that one cannot claim *justification* for the violation. It does not become *all right*.

As a tentative effort to explain this, let me try to connect absolutist limitations with the possibility of justifying *to the victim* what is being done to him. If one abandons a person in the course of rescuing several others from a fire or a sinking ship, one *could* say to him, "You understand, I have to leave you to save the others." Similarly, if one subjects an unwilling child to a painful surgical procedure, one can say to him, "If you could understand, you would realize that I am doing this to help you." One could *even* say, as one bayonets an enemy soldier, "It's either you or me." But one cannot really say while torturing a prisoner, "You understand, I have to pull out your fingernails because it is absolutely essential that we have the names of your confederates"; nor can one say to the victims of Hiroshima, "You understand, we have to incinerate you to provide the Japanese government with an incentive to surrender."

This does not take us very far, of course, since a utilitarian would presumably be willing to offer justifications of the latter sort to his victims, in cases where he thought they were sufficient. They are really justifications to the world at large, which the victim, as a reasonable man, would be expected to appreciate. However, there seems to me something wrong with this view, for it ignores the possibility that to treat someone else horribly puts you in a special relation to him, which may have to be defended in terms of other features of your relation to him. The suggestion needs much more development; but it may help us to understand how there may be requirements which are absolute in the sense that there can be no justification for violating them. If the justification for what one did to another person had to be such that it could be offered to him specifically, rather than just to the world at large, that would be a significant source of restraint.

If the account is to be deepened, I would hope for some results along the following lines. Absolutism is associated with a view of oneself as a small being interacting with others in a large world. The justifications it requires are primarily interpersonal. Utilitarianism is associated with a view of oneself as a benevolent bureaucrat distributing such benefits as one can control to countless other beings, with whom one may have various relations or none. The justifications it requires are primarily administrative. The argument between the two moral attitudes may depend on the relative priority of these two conceptions.[8]

VI

Some of the restrictions on methods of warfare which have been adhered to from time to time are to be explained by the mutual interests of the involved parties: restrictions on weaponry, treatment of prisoners, etc. But that is not all there is to it. The conditions of directness and relevance which I have argued apply to relations of conflict and aggression apply to war as well. I have said that there are two types of absolutist restrictions on the conduct of war: those that limit the legitimate targets of hostility and those that limit its character, even when the target is acceptable. I shall say something about each of these. As will become clear, the principle I have sketched does not yield an unambiguous answer in every case.

First let us see how it implies that attacks on some people are allowed, but not attacks on others. It may seem paradoxical to assert that to fire a machine gun at someone who is throwing hand grenades at your emplacement is to treat him as a human being. Yet the relation with him is direct and straightforward.[9] The attack is aimed specifically against the threat presented by a dangerous adversary, and not against a peripheral target through which he happens to be vulnerable but which has nothing to do with that threat. For example, you might stop him by machine-gunning his wife and children, who are standing nearby, thus distracting him from his aim of blowing you up and enabling you to capture him. But if his wife and children are not threatening your life, that would be to treat them as means with a vengeance.

8. Finally, I should mention a different possibility, suggested by Robert Nozick: that there is a strong general presumption against benefiting from the calamity of another, whether or not it has been deliberately inflicted for that or any other reason. This broader principle may well lend its force to the absolutist position.

9. It has been remarked that according to my view, shooting at someone establishes an I-thou relationship.

This, however, is just Hiroshima on a smaller scale. One objection to weapons of mass annihilation—nuclear, thermonuclear, biological, or chemical—is that their indiscriminateness disqualifies them as direct instruments for the expression of hostile relations. In attacking the civilian population, one treats neither the military enemy nor the civilians with that minimal respect which is owed to them as human beings. This is clearly true of the direct attack on people who present no threat at all. But it is also true of the character of the attack on those who *are* threatening you, viz., the government and military forces of the enemy. Your aggression is directed against an area of vulnerability quite distinct from any threat presented by them which you may be justified in meeting. You are taking aim at them through the mundane life and survival of their countrymen, instead of aiming at the destruction of their military capacity. And of course it does not require hydrogen bombs to commit such crimes.

This way of looking at the matter also helps us to understand the importance of the distinction between combatants and noncombatants, and the irrelevance of much of the criticism offered against its intelligibility and moral significance. According to an absolutist position, deliberate killing of the innocent is murder, and in warfare the role of the innocent is filled by noncombatants. This has been thought to raise two sorts of problems: first, the widely imagined difficulty of making a division, in modern warfare, between combatants and noncombatants; second, problems deriving from the connotation of the word "innocence."

Let me take up the latter question first.[10] In the absolutist position, the operative notion of innocence is not moral innocence, and it is not opposed to moral guilt. If it were, then we would be justified in killing a wicked but noncombatant hairdresser in an enemy city who supported the evil policies of his government, and unjustified in killing a morally pure conscript who was driving a tank toward us with the profoundest regrets and nothing but love in his heart. But moral innocence has very little to do with it, for in the definition of murder "innocent" means "currently harmless," and it is opposed not to "guilty" but to "doing harm." It should be noted that such an analysis has the consequence that in war we may often be justified in kill-

10. What I say on this subject derives from Anscombe.

ing people who do not deserve to die, and unjustified in killing people who do deserve to die, if anyone does.

So we must distinguish combatants from noncombatants on the basis of their immediate threat or harmfulness. I do not claim that the line is a sharp one, but it is not so difficult as is often supposed to place individuals on one side of it or the other. Children are not combatants even though they may join the armed forces if they are allowed to grow up. Women are not combatants just because they bear children or offer comfort to the soldiers. More problematic are the supporting personnel, whether in or out of uniform, from drivers of munitions trucks and army cooks to civilian munitions workers and farmers. I believe they can be plausibly classified by applying the condition that the prosecution of conflict must direct itself to the cause of danger, and not to what is peripheral. The threat presented by an army and its members does not consist merely in the fact that they are men, but in the fact that they are armed and are using their arms in the pursuit of certain objectives. Contributions to their arms and logistics are contributions to this threat; contributions to their mere existence as men are not. It is therefore wrong to direct an attack against those who merely serve the combatants' needs as human beings, such as farmers and food suppliers, even though survival as a human being is a necessary condition of efficient functioning as a soldier.

This brings us to the second group of restrictions: those that limit what may be done even to combatants. These limits are harder to explain clearly. Some of them may be arbitrary or conventional, and some may have to be derived from other sources; but I believe that the condition of directness and relevance in hostile relations accounts for them to a considerable extent.

Consider first a case which involves both a protected class of noncombatants and a restriction on the measures that may be used against combatants. One provision of the rules of war which is universally recognized, though it seems to be turning into a dead letter in Vietnam, is the special status of medical personnel and the wounded in warfare. It might be more efficient to shoot medical officers on sight and to let the enemy wounded die rather than be patched up to fight another day. But someone with medical insignia is supposed to be left alone and permitted to tend and retrieve the wounded. I believe this is because medical attention is a species of attention to completely general human needs, not specifically the needs of a combat soldier, and our conflict with the soldier is not with his existence as a human being.

By extending the application of this idea, one can justify prohibitions against certain particularly cruel weapons: starvation, poisoning, infectious diseases (supposing they could be inflicted on combatants only), weapons designed to maim or disfigure or torture the opponent rather than merely to stop him. It is not, I think, mere casuistry to claim that such weapons attack the men, not the soldiers. The effect of dum-dum bullets, for example, is much more extended than necessary to cope with the combat situation in which they are used. They abandon any attempt to discriminate in their effects between the combatant and the human being. For this reason the use of flamethrowers and napalm is an atrocity in all circumstances that I can imagine, whoever the target may be. Burns are both extremely painful and extremely disfiguring—far more than any other category of wound. That this well-known fact plays no (inhibiting) part in the determination of U.S. weapons policy suggests that moral sensitivity among public officials has not increased markedly since the Spanish Inquisition.[11]

11. Beyond this I feel uncertain. Ordinary bullets, after all, can cause death, and nothing is more permanent than that. I am not at all sure why we are justified in trying to kill those who are trying to kill us (rather than merely in trying to stop them with force which may also result in their deaths). It is often argued that incapacitating gases are a relatively humane weapon (when not used, as in Vietnam, merely to make people easier to shoot). Perhaps the legitimacy of restrictions against them must depend on the dangers of escalation, and the great utility of maintaining *any* conventional category of restriction so long as nations are willing to adhere to it.

Let me make clear that I do not regard my argument as a defense of the moral immutability of the Hague and Geneva Conventions. Rather, I believe that they rest partly on a moral foundation, and that modifications of them should also be assessed on moral grounds.

But even this connection with the actual laws of war is not essential to my claims about what is permissible and what is not. Since completing this paper I have read an essay by Richard Wasserstrom entitled "The Laws of War" (forthcoming in *The Monist*), which argues that the existing laws and conventions do not even attempt to embody a decent moral position: that their provisions have been determined by other interests, that they are in fact immoral

Finally, the same condition of appropriateness to the true object of hostility should limit the scope of attacks on an enemy country: its economy, agriculture, transportation system, and so forth. Even if the parties to a military conflict are considered to be not armies or governments but entire nations (which is usually a grave error), that does not justify one nation in warring against every aspect or element of another nation. That is not justified in a conflict between individuals, and nations are even more complex than individuals, so the same reasons apply. Like a human being, a nation is engaged in countless other pursuits while waging war, and it is not in those respects that it is an enemy.

The burden of the argument has been that absolutism about murder has a foundation in principles governing all one's relations to other persons, whether aggressive or amiable, and that these principles, and that absolutism, apply to warfare as well, with the result that certain measures are impermissible no matter what the consequences.[12] I do not mean to romanticize war. It is sufficiently utopian to suggest that when nations conflict they might rise to the level of limited barbarity that typically characterizes violent conflict between individuals, rather than wallowing in the moral pit where they appear to have settled, surrounded by enormous arsenals.

VII

Having described the elements of the absolutist position, we must now return to the conflict between it and utilitarianism. Even if certain types of dirty tactics become acceptable when the stakes are high enough, the most serious of the prohibited acts, like murder and torture, are not just supposed to require unusually strong justifica-

in substance, and that it is a grave mistake to refer to them as standards in forming moral judgments about warfare. This possibility deserves serious consideration, and I am not sure what to say about it, but it does not affect my view of the moral issues.

12. It is possible to draw a more radical conclusion, which I shall not pursue here. Perhaps the technology and organization of modern war are such as to make it impossible to wage as an acceptable form of interpersonal or even international hostility. Perhaps it is too impersonal and large-scale for that. If so, then absolutism would in practice imply pacifism, given the present state of things. On the other hand, I am skeptical about the unstated assumption that a technology dictates its own use.

tion. They are supposed *never* to be done, because no quantity of resulting benefit is thought capable of *justifying* such treatment of a person.

The fact remains that when an absolutist knows or believes that the utilitarian cost of refusing to adopt a prohibited course will be very high, he may hold to his refusal to adopt it, but he will find it difficult to feel that a moral dilemma has been satisfactorily resolved. The same may be true of someone who rejects an absolutist requirement and adopts instead the course yielding the most acceptable consequences. In either case, it is possible to feel that one has acted for reasons insufficient to justify violation of the opposing principle. In situations of deadly conflict, particularly where a weaker party is threatened with annihilation or enslavement by a stronger one, the argument for resorting to atrocities can be powerful, and the dilemma acute.

There may exist principles, not yet codified, which would enable us to resolve such dilemmas. But then again there may not. We must face the pessimistic alternative that these two forms of moral intuition are not capable of being brought together into a single, coherent moral system, and that the world can present us with situations in which there is no honorable or moral course for a man to take, no course free of guilt and responsibility for evil.

The idea of a moral blind alley is a perfectly intelligible one. It is possible to get into such a situation by one's own fault, and people do it all the time. If, for example, one makes two incompatible promises or commitments—becomes engaged to two people, for example—then there is no course one can take which is not wrong, for one must break one's promise to at least one of them. Making a clean breast of the whole thing will not be enough to remove one's reprehensibility. The existence of such cases is not morally disturbing, however, because we feel that the situation was not unavoidable: one had to do something wrong in the first place to get into it. But what if the world itself, or someone else's actions, could face a previously innocent person with a choice between morally abominable courses of action, and leave him no way to escape with his honor? Our intuitions rebel at the idea, for we feel that the constructibility of such a case must show a contradiction in our moral views. But it is not in itself a contradiction to say that someone can do X or not do X, and that for him to take either course would be wrong. It merely contradicts the supposition that *ought* implies *can*—since presumably one ought to refrain from what is wrong, and in such a case it is impossible to do so.[13] Given the limitations on human action, it is naïve to suppose that there is a solution to every moral problem with which the world can face us. We have always known that the world is a bad place. It appears that it may be an evil place as well.

13. This was first pointed out to me by Christopher Boorse.

R. B. BRANDT   Utilitarianism and the
                             Rules of War

The topic of the present symposium is roughly the moral proscriptions and prescriptions that should govern the treatment by a belligerent, and in particular by its armed forces, of the nationals of an
enemy, both combatants and noncombatants. In addressing myself to
it, the central question I shall try to answer is: What, from a moral
point of view, ought to be the rules of war? But this question, taken
as an indication of what I shall be discussing, is both too broad and
too narrow. Too broad because the rules of war include many topics
like the rights and duties of neutral countries and the proprieties pertaining to an armistice. And too narrow because a full view of the
topic requires me to consider, as I shall, such questions as: Is it ever
morally right for a person to infringe "ideal" rules of war?

I shall aim to illuminate our topic by discussing it from the point
of view of a rule-utilitarianism of the "contractual" variety (to use
a term employed by John Rawls in his book *A Theory of Justice*).[1]
What this point of view is has of course to be explained, as do the
special problems raised by the fact that the rules are to apply to nations at war. I believe it will become clear that the rule-utilitarian
viewpoint is a very helpful one for thinking of rules of warfare, and
I believe reflection on its implications will confirm us both in conclusions about certain normative rules and in a conviction that a
contractual utilitarian view of such matters is essentially sound.
Needless to say, I shall be led to express some disagreement with
Professor Nagel.

1. (Cambridge, Mass., 1971).

I. NAGEL'S ABSOLUTISM

I shall take Nagel to be defending, first, the general view that certain kinds of action are, from a moral point of view, absolutely out of bounds, no matter what the circumstances; and second, a specific prohibition that applies this principle to the area of our interest. (His first thesis makes it proper to call his view "absolutist," in the sense that some general moral prohibitions do not have prima facie force only but are binding without exception, indefeasible.) Now Nagel is tentative in his espousal of these two theses, and sometimes contends only that we have some moral intuitions of this sort and that a study of these will show "the complexity, and perhaps the incoherence" of our moral ideas. Indeed, he says he is offering only a "somewhat qualified defense of absolutism," and concedes that in extreme circumstances there may be exceptions to his absolutist principles after all. Where Nagel is committed definitely is to a criticism of utilitarianism; he speaks scathingly of "the abyss of utilitarian apologetics for large-scale murder." In view of Nagel's tentativeness, I think it fair to disassociate him from the positive view I wish to criticize, although I am *calling* it Nagel's "absolutism." This positive view is, however, the only definite proposal he puts forward, and if I am to consider critically any positive antiutilitarian view in connection with Nagel's essay, it has to be this one. At any rate, this view is one that somebody *might* hold, and is well worth discussing.

The first point I wish to make is that a rule-utilitarian may quite well agree with Nagel that certain kinds of action are morally out of bounds absolutely and no matter what the circumstances. Take, for instance, some of the rules of warfare recognized by the United States Army:

> It is especially forbidden . . . to declare that no quarter will be given. . . . It is especially forbidden . . . to kill or wound an enemy who, having laid down his arms, or having no longer means of defense, has surrendered at discretion. . . .

> It is especially forbidden . . . to employ arms, projectiles, or material calculated to cause unnecessary suffering. . . .

> The pillage of a town or place, even when taken by assault, is prohibited. . . .

A commander may not put his prisoners to death because their presence retards his movements or diminishes his power of re- sistance by necessitating a large guard, or by reason of their con- suming supplies, or because it appears certain that they will regain their liberty through the impending success of their forces. It is likewise unlawful for a commander to kill his prisoners on grounds of self-preservation, even in the case of airborne or commando operations, although the circumstances of the operation may make necessary rigorous supervision of and restraint upon the move- ment of prisoners of war.[2]

A rule-utilitarian is certainly in a position to say that utilitarian considerations cannot morally justify a departure from these rules; in that sense they are absolute. But he will of course also say that the moral justification of these rules lies in the fact that their acceptance and enforcement will make an important contribution to long-range utility. The rule-utilitarian, then, may take a two-level view: that in justifying the rules, utilitarian considerations are in order and noth- ing else is; whereas in making decisions about what to do in concrete circumstances, the rules are absolutely binding. In the rule-utilitarian view, immediate expediency is not a moral justification for infringing the rules.[3]

It is not clear that Nagel recognizes this sort of absolutism about "ideal" rules of war as a possible utilitarian view, but he seems to disagree with it when he claims that some moral prohibitions are entirely independent of utilitarian considerations.

2. Department of the Army Field Manual PM 27-10, *The Law of Land War- fare* (Department of the Army, July 1956), pp. 17, 18, 21, 35. The Manual specifically states that the rules of war may not be disregarded on grounds of "military necessity" (p. 4), since considerations of military necessity were fully taken into account in framing the rules. (All page numbers in the text refer to this publication, hereafter called the Army Manual.)

Other valuable discussions of contemporary rules of warfare are to be found in L. Oppenheim, *International Law*, ed. H. Lauterpacht, 7th edn. (New York, 1952) and in Marjorie M. Whiteman, *Digest of International Law*, esp. Vol. X (U.S. Department of State, 1963).

3. It is conceivable that ideal rules of war would include one rule to the effect that anything is allowable, if necessary to prevent absolute catastrophe. As Oppenheim remarks, it may be that if the basic values of society are threatened nations are possibly released from all the restrictions in order to do what "they deem to be decisive for the ultimate vindication of the law of nations" (*International Law*, p. 351).

What absolute rule, then, does Nagel propose? I shall formulate and criticize his proposal in a moment. But first we should note that his rule is intended to be restricted in scope; it applies only to what "we deliberately do to people." This is an important restriction. Suppose bombers are dispatched to destroy a munitions factory—surely a legitimate military target in a night raid; in fact and predictably, and from a military point of view incidentally, the bombs kill five thousand people. Is this a case of "deliberately doing" something to these people? Nagel's view here seems obscure. He rejects the law of double effect and says he prefers to "stay with the original, unanalyzed distinction between what one does to people and what merely happens to them as a result of what one does." He concedes that this distinction "needs clarification." Indeed it does. Without more clarification, Nagel is hardly giving an explicit theory. I note that the U.S. Army Manual appears to reject this distinction, and in a paragraph declaring the limitations on strategic bombing states that "loss of life and damage to property must not be out of proportion to the military advantage to be gained" (p. 19).

The absolutist principle that Nagel espouses as the basic restriction on legitimate targets and weapons is this: "hostility or aggression should be directed at its true object. This means both that it should be directed at the person or persons who provoke it and that it should aim more specifically at what is provocative about them. The second condition will determine what form the hostility may appropriately take." Now, while I find this principle reasonably clear in its application to simple two-person cases discussed by him, I find it difficult to apply in the identification of morally acceptable military operations. With some trepidation I suggest that Nagel intends it to be construed to assert something like the following for the case of military operations: "Persons may be attacked 'deliberately' only if their presence or their position prevents overpowering the military forces of the enemy in some way; and they may be attacked only in a manner that is reasonably related to the objective of disarming or disabling them." If this is what he has in mind it is still rather vague, since it does not make clear whether attacks on munitions factories are legitimate, or whether attacks on persons involved in supporting services, say, the provisioning of the army, are acceptable.

It is worth noting that a principle resembling this one might have a utilitarian justification of the kind alluded to above. But the principle standing by itself does not seem to me self-evident; nor does another principle Nagel asserts, that "the maintenance of a direct interpersonal response to the people one deals with is a requirement which no advantages can justify one in abandoning."

II. MORALLY JUSTIFIABLE RULES AS RULES IMPARTIALLY PREFERABLE

I shall now proceed to a positive account of the rules of war and of their justification. We shall have to consider several distinct questions, but the central question will be: Which of the possible rules of war are morally justifiable?

But first, what do I mean by "rules of war" or by talk of the "authoritative status" of rules of war? What I have in mind is, roughly, rules with the status that the articles of the Hague and Geneva Conventions have or have had. That is, certain rules pertaining to war are stated in formal treaties. These rules are seriously taught, as being legally binding, to officers and to some extent to enlisted men; they are recognized as legally binding restrictions on the decisions of the general staff; members of the army know that actions forbidden by these rules are contrary both to international law and to their own army's manual of rules for proper conduct; these rules are enforced seriously by the courts, either military or international; and so on. Proscriptions or prescriptions with this status I call "rules of war"; and in speaking of a rule having "authoritative status" I have this kind of force in mind. The U.S. Army Manual lists such rules; and digests of international law such as those by Whiteman and Oppenheim contain information on what such rules are and have been.

I have said that I shall offer a utilitarian answer to the question which rules of war (in the above sense) are morally justifiable. But I have also said that I shall be offering what I (following Rawls) call a *contractual* utilitarian answer. What I mean by that (the term "contractual" may be a bit misleading) is this. I accept the utilitarian answer to the question which rules of war are morally justifiable because utilitarian rules of war are the ones *rational, impartial persons would choose* (the ones they would be willing to put themselves under a contract to obey). The more basic question is, then: Which rules of war would people universally prefer to have accorded authoritative status among nations if the people deciding were rational, believed they might be involved in a war at some time, and were impartial in the sense that they were choosing behind a veil of ignorance? (It is understood that their ignorance is to be such as to prevent them from making a choice that would give them or their nation a special advantage; it would, for instance, prevent them from knowing what weaponry their country would possess were it to be at war, and from knowing whether, were war to occur, they would be on the front lines, in a factory, or in the general staff office.) In other words, the more fundamental question is: What rules would rational, impartial people, who expected their country at some time to be at war, want to have as the authoritative rules of war—particularly with respect to the permitted targets and method of attack? I suggest that the rules of war which rational, impartial persons would choose are the rules that would maximize long-range expectable utility for nations at war. In saying this I am offering a contractual utilitarian answer to the question what rules of war are morally justifiable. I am saying, then: (1) that rational, impartial persons would choose certain rules of war; (2) that I take as a basic premise ("analytic" in some sense, if you like) that a rule of war is morally justified if and only if it would be chosen by rational, impartial persons; and (3) that the rules rational, impartial persons would choose are ones which will maximize expectable long-range utility for nations at war.[4]

Nagel objects to utilitarianism and hence presumably would object to (3), but he might be agreeable to both (1) and (2). At least he seems close to these principles, since he seems to hold that an action is justified if one can justify to its victim what is being done to him. For instance, he implies that if you were to say to a prisoner, "You understand, I have to pull out your fingernails because it is absolutely essential that we have the name of your confederates" and the

4. This summary statement needs much explanation, e.g., regarding the meaning of "rational." It is only a close approximation to the view I would defend, since I think it is better to substitute a more complex notion for that of impartiality or a veil of ignorance.

prisoner agreed to this as following from principles he accepts, then the torture would be justified. Nagel rather assumes that the prisoner would not agree, in an appropriate sense. In this connection we must be clearly aware of an important distinction. A judge who sentences a criminal might also be unable to persuade the criminal to want the sentence to be carried out; and if persuading him to want this were necessary for a moral justification of the criminal law, then the system of criminal justice would also be morally objectionable. We must distinguish between persuading a person to whom something horrible is about to be done to want that thing to happen or to consent to its happening at that very time and something quite different—getting him to accept, when he is rational and choosing in ignorance of his own future prospects, some general principles from which it would follow that this horrible thing should or might be done to a person in his present circumstances. I think Nagel must mean, or ought to mean, that a set of rules of war must be such as to command the assent of rational people choosing behind a veil of ignorance, *not* that a person must be got to assent at the time to his fingernails being pulled out in order to get information, if that act is to be justified. It may be, however, that Nagel does not agree with this distinction, since he hints at the end of his discussion that something more may be required for moral justification than I have suggested, without indicating what the addition might be.

We should notice that the question which rules of war would be preferred by rational persons choosing behind a veil of ignorance is roughly the question that bodies like the Hague Conventions tried to answer. For there were the representatives of various nations, gathered together, say, in 1907, many or all of them making the assumption that their nations would at some time be at war. And, presumably in the light of calculated national self-interest and the principles of common humanity, they decided which rules they were prepared to commit themselves to follow, in advance of knowing how the fortunes of war might strike them in particular. The questions the signatories to the Hague Conventions actually did ask themselves are at least very close to the questions I think we must answer in order to know which rules of war are morally justified.

III. THE RATIONAL, IMPARTIAL CHOICE: UTILITARIAN RULES

I wish now to explain in a few words why I think rational, impartial persons would choose rules of war that would maximize expectable utility. Then—and this will occupy almost all of the present section—I shall classify the rules of war into several types, and try to show that representative rules of each type would be utility-maximizing and therefore chosen. I shall hope (although I shall not say anything explicitly about this) that the ideal rules of war, identified in this way, will coincide with the reflective intuitions of the reader. If so, I assume that this fact will commend to him the whole of what I am arguing.

I have suggested that rational persons, choosing behind a veil of ignorance but believing that their country may well be involved in a war at some time, would prefer rules of war that would maximize expectable utility, *in the circumstance that two nations are at war.* Why would they prefer such rules? About this I shall say only that if they are self-interested they will choose rules which will maximize expectable utility generally, for then their chance of coming out best will be greatest (and they do not know how especially to favor themselves); and that if they are altruistic they will again choose that set of rules, for they will want to choose rules which will maximize expectable utility generally. The rules of war, then, subject to the restriction that the rules of war may not prevent a belligerent from using all the power necessary to overcome the enemy, will be ones whose authorization will serve to maximize welfare.

It is worth noting that a preamble to the U.S. Army Manual offers an at least partially utilitarian theory of the rules of war (I say "at least partially" because of doubts about the interpretation of clause *b*). This preamble states that the law of land warfare "is inspired by the desire to diminish the evils of war by: *a.* Protecting both combatants and noncombatants from unnecessary suffering; *b.* Safeguarding certain fundamental human rights of persons who fall into the hands of the enemy, particularly prisoners of war, the wounded and sick, and civilians; and *c.* Facilitating the restoration of peace" (p. 3).

Which rules, then, would maximize expectable utility for nations at war? (I shall later discuss briefly whether the ideal rules would altogether forbid war as an instrument of national policy.)

First, however, we must understand why the above-mentioned restriction, guaranteeing that the rules of war will not prevent a belligerent from using all the force necessary to overcome the enemy, must be placed on the utility-maximizing rules of war. The reason for this restriction is to be found in the nature of a serious war. There are, of course, many different kinds of war. Wars differ in magnitude, in the technologies they employ, in the degree to which they mobilize resources, in the type of issue the belligerents believe to be at stake, and in many other ways as well. The difference between the Trojan War and World War II is obviously enormous. The former was a simple, small-scale affair, and the issues at stake might well have been settled by a duel between Paris and Menelaus, or Hector and Achilles, and the belligerents might not have been seriously dissatisfied with the outcome. In the case of World War II, the British thought that Hitler's Germany and its policies threatened the very basis of civilized society. The destruction of Hitler's power seemed so important to the British that they were willing to stake their existence as a nation on bringing it about. Wars have been fought for many lesser reasons: to spread a political or religious creed, to acquire territory or wealth, to obtain an outlet to the sea, or to become established as a world power. Wars may be fought with mercenaries, or primarily by the contribution of equipment and munitions; such wars make relatively little difference to the domestic life of a belligerent.

It is possible that the rules which would maximize expectable utility might vary from one type of war to another. I shall ignore this possibility for the most part, and merely note that practical difficulties are involved in equipping military handbooks with different sets of rules and establishing judicial bodies to identify the proper classification of a given war. I shall take the position of Britain in World War II as typical of that of a belligerent in a serious war.

The position of a nation in a serious war is such, then, that it considers overpowering the enemy to be absolutely vital to its interests (and possibly to those of civilized society generally)—so vital, indeed, that it is willing to risk its very existence to that end. It is doubtful that both sides can be well justified in such an appraisal of the state of affairs. But we may assume that in fact they do make this appraisal. In this situation, we must simply take as a fact that neither side will consent to or follow rules of war which seriously impair the possibility of bringing the war to a victorious conclusion. This fact accounts for the restriction within which I suggested a choice of the rules of war must take place. We may notice that the recognized rules of war do observe this limitation: they are framed in such a way as not to place any serious obstacle in the way of a nation's using any available force, if necessary, to destroy the ability of another to resist. As Oppenheim has observed, one of the assumptions underlying the recognized rules of war is that "a belligerent is justified in applying any amount and any kind of force which is necessary for . . . the overpowering of the opponent."[5] This limitation, however, leaves a good deal of room for rules of war which will maximize expectable long-range utility for all parties.

This restriction, incidentally, itself manifests utilitarian considerations, for a nation is limited to the use of means *necessary* to overcome an opponent. Clearly it is contrary to the general utility that any amount or manner of force be employed when it is *not* necessary for victory.

It will be convenient to divide the rules restricting military operation, especially the targets and weapons of attack, into three types. (I do not claim that these are exhaustive.)

1. *Humanitarian restrictions of no cost to military operation.* There are some things that troops may be tempted to do which are at best of negligible utility to their nation but which cause serious loss to enemy civilians, although not affecting the enemy's power to win the war. Such behavior will naturally be forbidden by rules designed to maximize expectable utility within the understood restriction. Consider, for example, rules against the murder or ill-treatment of prisoners of war. A rule forbidding wanton murder of prisoners hardly needs discussion. Such murder does not advance the war effort of the captors; indeed, news of its occurrence only

5. *International Law*, p. 226.

stiffens resistance and invites retaliation. Moreover, there is an advantage in returning troops having been encouraged to respect the lives of others. A strict prohibition of wanton murder of prisoners therefore has the clear support of utilitarian considerations. Much the same may be said for a rule forbidding ill-treatment of prisoners. There can, of course, be disagreement about what constitutes ill-treatment—for instance, whether a prisoner is entitled to a diet of the quality to which he is accustomed if it is more expensive than that available to troops of the captor army. It is clear, however, that in a war between affluent nations prisoners can generally be well-housed and well-fed and receive adequate medical care without cost to the war effort of the captors. And if they receive such treatment, of course the captives gain. Thus a policy of good treatment of prisoners may be expected to make many nationals of both sides better off, and at a cost which in no way impairs the ability of either to wage the war.

Again, much the same may be said of the treatment of civilians and of civilian property in occupied territories. There is no military advantage, at least for an affluent nation, in the plunder of private or public property. And the rape of women or the ill-treatment of populations of occupied countries serves no military purpose. On the contrary, such behavior arouses hatred and resentment and constitutes a military liability. So utility is maximized, within our indicated basic limitations, by a strict rule calling for good treatment of the civilian population of an occupied territory. And the same can be said more generally for the condemnation of the wanton destruction of cities, towns, or villages, or devastation not justified by military necessity, set forth in the Charter of the Nuremberg Tribunal.

Obviously these rules, which the maximization of expectable utility calls for, are rules that command our intuitive assent.

2. *Humanitarian restrictions possibly costly to military victory.* Let us turn now to rules pertaining to actions in somewhat more complex situations. There are some actions which fall into neither of the classes so far discussed. They are not actions which must be permitted because they are judged necessary or sufficient for victory, and hence actions on which no party to a major war would ac-

cept restrictions. Nor are they actions which morally justified rules of war definitely prohibit, as being actions which cause injury to enemy nationals but serve no military purpose. It is this large class of actions neither clearly permitted nor definitely prohibited, for reasons already discussed, that I wish now to consider. I want to ask which rules of war are morally justified, because utility-maximizing, for actions of this kind. In what follows I shall be distinguishing several kinds of action and suggesting appropriate rules for them. The first type is this: doing something which will result in widespread destruction of civilian life and property and at the same time will add (possibly by that very destruction) to the *probability* of victory but will not definitely decide the war. Some uses of atomic weapons, and area bombing of the kind practiced at Hamburg, illustrate this sort of case.

A proper (not ideally precise) rule for such operations might be: substantial destruction of lives and property of enemy civilians is permissible only when there is good evidence that it will significantly enhance the prospect of victory. Application of the terms "good evidence" and "significantly enhance" requires judgment, but the rule could be a useful guideline all the same. For instance, we now know that the destruction of Hamburg did not significantly enhance the prospect of victory; in fact, it worked in the wrong direction, since it both outraged the population and freed workers formerly in non-war-supporting industries to be moved into industry directly contributing to the German war effort. The generals surely did not have good evidence that this bombing would significantly enhance the prospect of victory.

This rule is one which parties to a war might be expected to accept in advance, since following it could be expected to minimize the human cost of war on both sides, and since it does not involve a significant compromise of the goal of victory. The proposed rule, incidentally, has some similarities to the accepted rule cited above from the U.S. Army Manual, that "loss of life and damage to property must not be out of proportion to the military advantage to be gained."

This rule, which I am suggesting only for wars like World War II, where the stakes are very high, may become clearer if seen in the perspective of a more general rule that would also be suitable for wars in which the stakes are much lower. I pointed out above that what is at stake in a war may be no more than a tiny strip of land or national prestige. (The utility of these, may, however, be considered very great by a nation.) Now, it is clear that a risk of defeat which may properly be taken when the stakes are small may not be a proper risk when the stakes are virtually infinite; and a risk that could not properly be run when the stakes are enormous might quite properly be run when the stakes are small. So if the above-suggested rule is plausible for serious wars, in which the stakes are great, a somewhat different rule will be plausible in the case of wars of lesser importance—one that will require more in the way of "good evidence" and will require that the actions more "significantly enhance" the prospect of victory than is necessary when the stakes are much higher. These thoughts suggest the following general principle, applicable to all types of war: a military action (e.g., a bombing raid) is permissible only if the utility (broadly conceived, so that the maintenance of treaty obligations of international law could count as a utility) of victory to all concerned, multiplied by the increase in its probability if the action is executed, on the evidence (when the evidence is reasonably solid, considering the stakes), is greater than the possible disutility of the action to both sides multiplied by its probability. The rule for serious wars suggested above could then be regarded as a special case, one in which the utility of victory is virtually set at infinity—so that the only question is whether there is reasonably solid evidence that the action will increase the probability of victory. The more general rule obviously involves difficult judgments; there is a question, therefore, as to how it could be applied. It is conceivable that tough-minded civilian review boards would be beneficial, but we can hardly expect very reliable judgments even from them.[6]

6. If we assume that both sides in a major struggle somehow manage to be persuaded that their cause is just, we shall have to expect that each will assign a net positive utility to its being the victor. For this reason it makes very little difference whether the more general principle uses the concept of the utility of victory by one side for everyone concerned, or the utility for that side only.

One might propose that the general restriction on rules of war, to the effect that in a serious war the use of any force necessary or sufficient for victory

These rules are at least very different from a blanket permission for anything the military thinks might conceivably improve the chances of victory, irrespective of any human cost to the enemy. In practice, it must be expected that each party to a war is likely to estimate the stakes of victory quite high, so that the rule which has the best chance of being respected is probably the first one mentioned, and not any modification of it that would be suggested to an impartial observer by the second, more general principle.

The reader may have been struck by the fact that these suggested rules are essentially institutionalized applications of a kind of act-utilitarian principle for certain contexts. This may seem inconsistent with the notion of a system of absolute rules themselves justified by long-range utilitarian considerations. But there is nothing inconsistent in the suggestion that some of the "absolute" rules should require that in certain situations an action be undertaken if and only if it will maximize expectable utility.

It may be objected that the rules suggested are far too imprecise to be of practical utility. To this I would reply that there is no reason why judgment may not be required in staff decisions about major operations. Furthermore, the U.S. Army Manual already contains several rules the application of which requires judgment. For example:

> Absolute good faith with the enemy must be observed as a rule of conduct. . . . In general, a belligerent may resort to those measures for mystifying or misleading the enemy against which the enemy ought to take measures to protect himself.

> The measure of permissible devastation is found in the strict necessities of war. Devastation as an end in itself or as a separate

---

must be permitted, might be derived from the above principle if the utility of victory is set virtually at infinity and the probability of a certain action affecting the outcome is set near one. I believe this is correct, if we assume, as just suggested, that each side in a serious war will set a very high positive utility on *its* being the victor, despite the fact that both sides cannot possibly be correct in such an assessment. The reason for this principle as stated in the text, however, seems to me more realistic and simple. There is no reason, as far as I can see, why *both* lines of reasoning may not be used in support of the claim that the principle (or restriction) in question is a part of a morally justifiable system of rules of war.

measure of war is not sanctioned by the law of war. There must be some reasonably close connection between the destruction of property and the overcoming of the enemy's army. . . .

The punishment imposed for a violation of the law of war must be proportionate to the gravity of the offense. The death penalty may be imposed for grave breaches of the law. . . . Punishments should be deterrent . . . (pp. 22, 23-24, 182).

It has sometimes been argued, for instance by Winston Churchill, that obliteration bombing is justified as retaliation. It has been said that since the Germans destroyed Amsterdam and Coventry, the British had a right to destroy Hamburg. And it is true that the Hague Conventions are sometimes regarded as a contract, breach of which by one side releases the other from its obligations. It is also true that a government which has itself ordered obliteration bombing is hardly in a position to complain if the same tactic is employed by the enemy. But maximizing utility permits obliteration bombing only as a measure of deterrence or deterrent reprisal. This rule, incidentally, is recognized by the Army Manual as a principle governing all reprisals: "Reprisals are acts of retaliation . . . for the purpose of enforcing future compliance with the recognized rules of civilized warfare. . . . Other means of securing compliance with the law of war should normally be exhausted before resort is had to reprisals. . . . Even when appeal to the enemy for redress has failed, it may be a matter of policy to consider, before resorting to reprisals, whether the opposing forces are not more likely to be influenced by a steady adherence to the law of war on the part of the adversary" (p. 177). Purposes of retaliation, then, do not permit bombing in contravention of the suggested general principles.

Special notice should be taken that widespread civilian bombing might be defended by arguing that a significant deterioration in civilian morale could bring an end to a war by producing internal revolution. Our principle does not exclude the possibility of such reasoning, in the presence of serious evidence about civilian morale, when the stakes of victory are high. But we know enough about how bombing affects civilian morale to know that such bombing could be justified only rarely, if at all. The U.S. Army seems to go further than this; its rule asserts that any attack on civilians "for the sole purpose of terrorizing the civilian population is also forbidden."[7] It may be, however, that in actual practice this rule is interpreted in such a way that it is identical with the less stringent rule which is as much as utilitarian considerations can justify; if not, I fear we have to say that at this point the Army's theory has gone somewhat too far.

3. *Acceptance of military losses for humanitarian reasons.* Let us now turn to some rules which have to do with what we might call the *economics* of warfare, when the ultimate outcome is not involved, either because the outcome is already clear or because the action is fairly local and its outcome will not have significant repercussions. What damage may one inflict on the enemy in order to cut one's own losses? For instance, may one destroy a city in order to relieve a besieged platoon, or in order to avoid prolonging a war with consequent casualties? (The use of atom bombs in Japan may be an instance of this type of situation.) It is convenient to deal with two types of cases separately.

First, when may one inflict large losses on the enemy in order to avoid smaller losses for oneself, given that the issue of the war is not in doubt? A complicating fact is that when the issue is no longer in doubt it would seem that the enemy ought to concede, thereby avoiding losses to both sides. Why fight on when victory is impossible? (Perhaps to get better terms of peace.) But suppose the prospective loser is recalcitrant. May the prospective victor then unleash any horrors whatever in order to terminate the war quickly or reduce his losses? It is clear that the superior power should show utmost patience and not make the terms of peace so severe as to encourage further resistance. On the other hand, long-range utility is not served if the rules of war are framed in such a way as to provide an umbrella for the indefinite continuation of a struggle by an inferior power. So it must be possible to inflict losses heavy enough to produce capitulation but not so heavy as to be out of proportion to the estimated cost of further struggle to both sides. This condition is especially important in view of the fact that in practice there will almost always be other pressures that can be brought to bear. The

7. Whiteman, *Digest of International Law*, X, 135.

application of such a rule requires difficult judgments, but some such rule appears called for by long-range utilitarian considerations.

The second question is: Should there be restrictions on the treatment of an enemy in the case of local actions which could hardly affect the outcome of the war, when these may cause significant losses? Rules of this sort are in fact already in force. For instance, as mentioned above, the Army Manual forbids killing of prisoners when their presence retards one's movements, reduces the number of men available for combat, uses up the food supply, and in general is inimical to the integrity of one's troops. Again, the Second Hague Convention forbids forcing civilians in occupied territory to give information about the enemy, and it forbids reprisals against the general civilian population "on account of the acts of individuals for which they cannot be regarded as jointly and severally responsible."[8] The taking of hostages is prohibited (Army Manual, p. 107).

All these rules prescribe that a belligerent be prepared to accept certain military disadvantages for the sake of the lives and welfare of civilians and prisoners. The disadvantages in question are not, however, losses that could be so serious as to affect the outcome of a war. Furthermore, the military gains and losses are ones which are likely to be evenly distributed, so that neither side stands to gain a long-term advantage if the rules are observed by both. So, without affecting the outcome of the war and without giving either side an unfair advantage, a considerable benefit can come to both belligerents in the form of the welfare of their imprisoned and occupied populations. Thus the long-run advantage of both parties is most probably served if they accept forms of self-restraint which can work out to be costly in occasional instances. Such rules will naturally be accepted by rational, impartial people in view of their long-range benefits.

IV. RULES OF WAR AND MORALITY

I have been arguing that there is a set of rules governing the conduct of warfare which rational, impartial persons who believed that their country might from time to time be engaged in a war would prefer to any alternative sets of rules and to the absence of

8. Article L.

rules. I have also suggested, although without argument, that it is proper to say of such a set of rules that it is morally justified (and of course I think that such a set ought to be formally recognized and given authoritative status). There is thus a fairly close parallel with the prohibitions (and justifications and recognized excuses) of the criminal law: certain of these would be preferred to alternative sets and to an absence of legal prohibitions by rational, impartial persons; the prohibitions that would be so preferred may (I think) be said to be morally justified; and such rules ought to be adopted as the law of the land. I do not say the parallel is exact.

It may be suggested that there will be a considerable discrepancy between what is permitted by such "morally justifiable" rules of war and what it is morally permissible for a person to do in time of war. (Nagel mentions dropping the bomb on Hiroshima, attacks on trucks bringing up food, and the use of flamethrowers in any situation whatever as examples of actions not morally permissible; but it is not clear that he would say these would be permitted by morally justifiable rules of war, or even that he recognizes a distinction between what is morally permissible and what is permitted by morally justifiable rules of war.) Moreover, it might be thought that such "morally justifiable" rules of war could not be derived from justified moral principles. It might be asked, too, what the moral standing of these "morally justified" rules of war is, in view of the fact that the rules of war actually accepted and in force may, at least in some particulars, be rather different. These are difficult questions, about which I wish to say something.

It is obvious that there may well be discrepancies between what a person morally may do in wartime and what is permitted by morally justified rules of war, just as there are discrepancies between what is morally permitted and what is permitted by morally justifiable rules of the criminal law. For one thing, the rules of war, like the criminal law, must be formulated in such a way that it is decidable whether a person has violated them; it must be possible to produce evidence that determines the question and removes it from the realm of speculation. More important, just as there are subtle inter-personal relations—such as justice and self-restraint in a family—which it is undesirable for the criminal law to attempt to regulate

but which may be matters of moral obligation, so there may well
be moral obligations controlling relations between members of belligerent armies which the rules of war cannot reach. For instance,
one might be morally obligated to go to some trouble or even take a
certain risk in order to give aid to a wounded enemy, but the rules
of war could hardly prescribe doing so. I am unable to think of a
case in which moral principles require a person to do what is forbidden by morally justifiable rules of war; I suppose this is possible.
But it is easy to think of cases in which moral principles forbid a
person to injure an enemy, or require him to aid an enemy, when
morally justifiable rules of war do not prescribe accordingly and
when the military law even forbids the morally required behavior.
(Consider, for instance, the fact that, according to the Manual, the
U.S. Army permits severe punishment for anyone who "without
proper authority, knowingly harbors or protects or gives intelligence
to, or communicates or corresponds with or holds any intercourse
with the enemy, either directly or indirectly . . ." [p. 33].)

The possible contrast between morally justifiable rules of war and
what is morally permitted will seem quite clear to persons with
firm moral intuitions. It may be helpful, however, to draw the contrast by indicating what it would be, at least for one kind of rule-
utilitarian theory of moral principles. A rule-utilitarian theory of
morality might say that what is morally permissible is any action
that would not be forbidden by the kind of conscience which would
maximize long-rang expectable utility were it built into people as an
internal regulator of their relations with other sentient beings, as
contrasted with other kinds of conscience or not having a conscience
at all. Then justifiable rules of war (with the standing described
above) would be one thing; what is morally permissible, in view of
ideal rules of conscience, might be another. Rational, impartial
persons, understanding that their country may be involved in a war,
might want one set of rules as rules of war, whereas rational, impartial persons choosing among types of conscience might want a
different and discrepant set of rules as rules of conscience. In the
same way there may be a discrepancy between a morally justified
system of criminal law and morally justified rules of conscience.
And just as, consequently, there may occasionally be a situation in

which it is one's moral duty to violate the criminal law, so there may occasionally be a situation in which it is one's moral duty to violate morally justifiable rules of war.

It might be asked whether a person who subscribed to sound moral principles would, if given the choice, opt for a system of rules of war; and if so, whether he would opt for a set that would maximize expectable utility for the situation of nations at war. I suggest that he would do so; that such a person would realize that international law, like the criminal law, has its place in human society, that not all decisions can simply be left to the moral intuitions of the agent, and that the rules of war and military justice are bound to be somewhat crude. He would opt for that type of system which will do the most good, given that nations will sometimes go to war. I am, however, only *suggesting* that he would; in order to show that he would one would have to identify the sound moral principles which would be relevant to such a decision.

Another question that might be raised is whether a person should follow the actual military rules of his country or the morally justifiable ones (in the sense explained above). This question can obviously be taken in either of two ways. If the question is which rules are legally binding, of course the actual rules of war recognized at present are legally binding on him. But the question might be: Is a person morally bound to follow the "ideal" rules of war, as compared with the actual ones (or the legal orders of his officer), if they come into conflict? Here two possible situations must be distinguished. It is logically possible that a morally justifiable set of rules of war would permit damage to the enemy more severe than would the actual rules of war; in that case, assuming the actual rules of war have the status of an obligation fixed by a treaty, the moral obligation would seem to be to follow the provisions of the treaty (subject to the usual difficulties about older treaties not contemplating contemporary situations). Suppose, however, that a superior officer commands one to do something that is permitted by the actual rules of war (that is, not explicitly forbidden) but which clearly would be forbidden by morally justifiable rules of war. The question is then whether a moral person would refuse to do what is permitted by an unjust institution but would be forbidden by a just one. It would have to be argued in detail that sound moral principles would not permit a person to do what would be permitted only by an unjust institution. I shall not attempt to argue the matter, but only suggest that sound moral principles would *not* permit obedience to an order forbidden by morally justifiable rules of war. It is quite possible, incidentally, contrary to what I have just said about the legal issues, that a court-martial would not succeed in convicting a person who refused an order of this sort and defended his action along these lines.

There is space only to advert to the larger issue of the moral justification for nations being belligerents at all. Presumably, just as there are morally justified rules of war, in the sense of rules which rational, impartial persons would choose on the assumption their country might be involved in a war, so there are morally justified rules about engaging in a war at all, in the sense of rules governing the behavior of nations which rational, impartial persons would subscribe to if they believed that they would live in a world in which the chosen rules might obtain. Not only are there such morally justified rules regarding belligerency, but almost every nation is in fact signatory to a treaty abjuring war as an instrument of policy. Moreover, it has been declared criminal by the Treaty of London for a person to plan, prepare, initiate, or wage a war of aggression or a war in violation of international treaties, agreements, or assurances. So there is basis both in morally justified principles of international law and in actual international law for questioning the position of a belligerent. Presumably the relation between these and the moral obligations of citizens and government officials is complex, rather parallel to that just described for the case of rules of war.

Rules of War and Moral Reasoning

I shall be content to add a few methodological notes to this consideration of the rules of war.[1] My reason for wishing to do so is that
I find the contrast between the methods of the two writers both
striking and instructive, and am convinced that a decision between
the two methods is of immense practical importance, because what
philosophy has to contribute to practical questions *is* simply a method
of discussing them rationally; and on the soundness of the method
will depend the rationality of the discussion.

I have the same difficulty as Brandt evidently had in believing
that Nagel is really wedded to the "absolutism" that he expounds in
his article; but since it is a kind of position which undoubtedly has
adherents, and indeed has superficial attractions, it is worthwhile
trying to be clear what is wrong with it. For brevity, I shall be referring to the "absolutist" whose views are set out in Nagel's paper as
"Nagel." But before I start doing this, some remarks about what I
take to be the predicament of the real Nagel may be in place.

This real person seems to be torn between two ways of moral thinking which he dubs "utilitarian" and "absolutist." That is to say, he
wants sometimes to use utilitarian arguments, with all their consid-

---

© R. M. Hare 1972

1. When I formed the intention of replying to Professor Nagel's paper, I
had not seen Professor Brandt's. The basis of Brandt's argument is so like
that which I should have adopted, and his conclusions coincide with my own
with so few exceptions that it would be pointless for me to go over the argument again, even if I could rival Brandt's clarity.

eration of the consequences for good or ill of alternative courses of action; but sometimes he wants to override such considerations with an absolute ban, founded upon simple general rules, on certain kinds of actions. We must note that Brandt also wishes to operate both with simple general rules and with calculations about consequences; both the real Nagel and he, therefore, have on their hands the problem of reconciling the two ways of thinking (which might, it seems, come into conflict). My verdict will be that, whereas Brandt has a way of dealing with this problem, the real Nagel has conspicuously failed to provide one. That is why, although halfway through his paper, when flirting with the law of double effect, he claims it as a merit of that device that it avoids the problem that in certain cases "nothing one could do would be morally permissible," at the end of the paper he admits that his own position has this same consequence. Absolutism, or an impure absolutism which tries to incorporate utilitarian elements without coherently relating them to its own absolutist structure, is bound to have this trouble.

IT MAY help to clarify these obscure remarks if I start by summarizing five theories about the basis of moral thought which have been current recently, one of which I have advocated myself. I shall argue that *for practical purposes* there is no important difference between these theories as regards the method of moral thinking which they generate—that they are, if I may be allowed to use a deplorably vague expression, practically equivalent. If, as I think, the version which I have advocated can be shown to have a basis in the logic of the moral concepts themselves,[2] and if this basis needs the addition of no substantial *moral* assumptions, this will provide equally strong support for all the other versions, since they do not differ from it in any respect which would deprive them of this support. I hope to show that the conclusions which Brandt has reached could be that much more firmly based if they were to rest on this foundation.

I shall call the five positions: (1) the ideal observer theory; (2) the rational contractor theory; (3) specific rule-utilitarianism; (4) universalistic act-utilitarianism; (5) universal prescriptivism. My bald summaries of these positions will be far from representing accurately

2. See my *Freedom and Reason* (Oxford, 1963), chaps. 6ff.

the views of any particular thinkers (even Brandt's and my own).
(1), (2), and (3), as I shall summarize them, bear a certain relation
(which is not one of identity) to theories which Brandt has advocated
in the past or in this symposium, and (4) is, as I have argued elsewhere, and as Professor David Lyons has argued more rigorously,
equivalent to (3). Mr. David Richards has expounded a theory of
type (2), and he, in turn, is heavily influenced by Professor Rawls's
views, although I hesitate even to summarize the latter until I have
read *A Theory of Justice*, which at the time of writing is still unpub-
lished.[3] Many other writers both in the past and recently have put forward theories which approximate to one or another of these types. A
clear display of their practical equivalence would therefore be of some
significance for moral philosophy, and have practical moral implications far beyond the issue of war and massacre raised by Nagel.

The ideal observer theory (as I shall summarize it) holds that in
considering what we ought to do, we have to conform our thought
to what would be said by a person who had access to complete knowledge of all the facts, was absolutely clear in his thinking, was impartial between all the parties affected by the action, and yet equally
benevolent to them all. That is to say, we are to think like a person
who gives equal, and positive, weight to the interests of all the parties
and to nothing else, and in serving these makes no factual or conceptual errors.

The rational contractor theory (in the version I shall discuss)
holds that what we ought to do is to follow those principles which
would be adopted by a set of rational people, each prudently considering his own interest, who were seeking agreement with each other on
the principles which should govern their conduct in a society of which
they were to be members; these rational contractors are presumed to
have complete knowledge of all facts about the society and the en-
vironment in which they are to live, *except* the particular role which is
to be played by each individual one of them.

3. R. B. Brandt, "The Definition of an 'Ideal Observer' Theory in Ethics,"
Philosophy and Phenomenological Research 15, no. 3 (1955): 407-413, and
Ethical Theory (Englewood Cliffs, N.J., 1959); David Lyons, *Forms and Limits
of Utilitarianism* (Oxford, 1965), chaps. 3-4; D.A.J. Richards, *A Theory of
Reasons for Action* (Oxford, 1971); John Rawls, *A Theory of Justice* (Cam-
bridge, Mass., 1971).

It is easy to see that these two theories are practically equivalent. For, firstly, the requirement of knowledge of the facts is common to both theories. The ideal observer, it is true, has access to one sort of fact of which the rational contractors have to be ignorant—namely the role which each individual plays. But this will make no difference, because the ideal observer, being required to be impartial between individuals, can make no use of this extra piece of knowledge in his moral thinking. Secondly, we may presume that the rational contractors, being rational, will, like the ideal observer, make no conceptual errors. Thirdly, the requirement that the ideal observer be impartial between individuals is exactly matched by the requirement that the rational contractors be ignorant of the individual roles which they are to play. For to be impartial (in the sense in which I shall be using the term) is to take no account of individuals qua those individuals; and it makes no difference whether this is done because of a direct requirement that no account be taken, or because no account *can* be taken owing to ignorance of which individual is to play which role. And lastly, the requirement that the ideal observer be benevolent is matched by the requirement that the rational contractors be prudent. We have already seen that both will give equal weight to the interests of all parties; that this equal weight will be positive is guaranteed in the one case by express stipulation, and in the other by the requirement that the rational contractors be prudent, i.e., consider their own interests. This, in conjunction with equality of weight, entails impartial *benevolence*.

It might be objected that the rational contractor theory introduces the notion of *principles* to be followed, whereas the ideal observer theory does not. But it does by implication. If no account is to be taken of individual (as opposed to qualitative) differences, the ideal observer will have to make his moral judgments in the form of principles expressed in purely universal terms; any individual name that occurred in them would have to be excluded as an irrelevancy. We see here how the feature of moral judgments which position (5) makes explicit, namely universalizability, is implicitly, but essentially, a feature of (1) and (2). As we shall see in a moment, it is also a feature of (3) and (4), which we must consider next.

I mean by *specific* rule-utilitarianism a type of rule-utilitarianism whose rules (or principles, as I prefer to call them) are allowed to be of unlimited specificity provided that they do not cease to be universal.[4] It is thus the practical equivalent of (4), namely an act-utilitarianism which accepts the meta-ethical view that moral judgments are universalizable. Positions (3) and (4) are practically equivalent, because (4), in accepting universalizability, admits that moral judgments made (on a utilitarian basis) about individual acts commit their maker also to principles applying to all precisely similar acts; and this is tantamount to accepting *specific* rule-utilitarianism. I shall therefore not deal with (4) separately. (3) holds that we ought on any occasion to do that act which is required by the set of principles whose universal observance would best serve the interests of all. For reasons given by Lyons, it will be possible for an act-utilitarian to force such a rule-utilitarian, since his principles *can* be as specific as he pleases, to *make* them specific enough to suit the particularities of each individual case; thus, again, (3) collapses into (4), as well as vice versa.

It now looks plausible to say that (3) and (4) come for practical purposes to the same thing as (1) and (2). I think that this is so, although the problem of distributive justice, to be mentioned shortly, might make me qualify this claim. The similarities, in any case, are obvious. The requirements of factual knowledge and of conceptual clarity are there as before; for one cannot successfully undertake utilitarian calculations without both of these. This is not to say that it is no use *trying* to do them unless one is perfect in these respects; here, as in the case of the first two theories, we are told what moral thought would be if done correctly, and enjoined to aim at this (though, as we shall see, a big practical qualification is needed here). The requirement of impartiality has been a part of utilitarianism at least since Bentham's "Everybody to count as one and nobody as more than one"; and these varieties are no exception, since impartiality is guaranteed by the stipulation that the principles must be universal. They cannot even mention individuals. The requirement of benevolence is secured by the reference to serving the interests of all.

4. For the distinction between generality (the opposite of specificity) and universality, see *Freedom and Reason*, pp. 38f., and my paper "Reasons of State" in my *Applications of Moral Philosophy* (forthcoming).

Coming now to the universal prescriptivist theory, we can see that it exhibits, in perhaps the clearest form of all, the essential features of the other four theories. It holds, on the basis of its analysis of the moral concepts, that when I am making up my mind what I ought to do, I am making up my mind what to prescribe for all cases exactly like this one in their universal properties. It should be evident that if this is what I am doing, I shall have to find out, first of all, just what I *am*, in effect, prescribing. This entails arming myself with the factual knowledge of what I should be bringing about if I acted upon one or another of the prescriptions between which I am deciding. It is part of this theory, too, that conceptual clarity is a necessary condition of rational moral thought.[5] Impartiality is guaranteed by the fact that my prescription has to apply to all cases resembling this one in their universal properties; since these will include cases (hypothetical or actual) in which I myself play the roles of each of the other parties affected, I am put by this theory in exactly the same position as the rational contractors. And benevolence is secured by the element of prescriptivity. Since I am prescribing actions which will affect the interests of myself and of others, and am bound to treat the interests of others as of equal weight to my own, we may presume that this weight will be at least positive. I shall not inquire here whether this last presumption could be defended a priori.

THIS IS hardly the place to elaborate and defend the five theories that I have been trying to merge with one another. Nor shall I even ask what other theories might also be merged with them, though it is obviously tempting to suggest that by making God the ideal observer (as in effect Butler does) some varieties of theological ethics could be brought in. It is worth mentioning, however, that there are at least four difficulties which all five of these theories have to face, and that this lends some support to my proposed merger. Three of these difficulties I shall simply list; but I shall deal at greater length with the fourth, since it has a close bearing on the dispute between Brandt and Nagel.

The first difficulty is that presented by the problem of distributive justice. So far, we do not know what the ideal observer, or the rational

5. See *Freedom and Reason*, esp. p. 185.

contractors, or I when I am universally prescribing will do when we are faced with a choice between maximizing benefits and distributing them in other ways which, though reducing their total, might be thought preferable for other reasons (for example, on grounds of fairness). Various such ways have been suggested—e.g., equality, the Pareto principle, and the maximin principle. Mr. Richards has not convinced me that there is a unique answer to the question of what the rational contractors would do when faced with such a choice (it might depend on how much gambling instinct they had); and the ideal observer is in the same trouble, as is the universal prescriber.[6]

It has been traditional among utilitarians to say that benefits should be maximized whatever their distribution; and this puts them at variance not only with common opinion, but with some exponents of the other kinds of theory—(1), (2), and (5)—that I have been summarizing. It might therefore be objected to my proposed merger that the five theories are not even practically equivalent, since (3) and (4)—the utilitarian theories—are committed to a particular answer to the question about distributive justice, whereas for the other theories the question at least remains open. My own tentative view is that it will not remain open once the implications of the three nonutilitarian theories have been fully understood, but that they too will be bound to accept the answer which requires maximization of benefits, though this answer will be qualified, and at the same time brought more into accord with received opinion, by the moves which I shall shortly make in discussing the fourth difficulty. I shall not try to defend this view here.

The second difficulty is that of justifying the enterprise of moral thought in the first place: What are we to say to the amoralist who just will not use the language whose logic requires him to reason in this way? The third difficulty is that presented by the fanatic who is prepared to prescribe universally that some particular ideal or goal of his should be realized at the expense of all other interests of himself and others. Both these difficulties affect all five theories—the second difficulty obviously, the third less obviously. But we can see that the third does affect the other four as much as it affects universal prescriptivism, if we consider that to have a fanatical ideal is to have

6. See *Freedom and Reason*, pp. 121f.

an interest in its realization. If the fanatic's interest in the realization of his ideal is great enough to trouble the universal prescriptivist, it will be great enough to claim a preponderant weight in the calculations of all the other four theories. All five theories will have to be content to say that fanatics of such heroic stature are unlikely ever to be encountered.[7] But I shall not pursue this argument here.

THE fourth difficulty, however, is one which must be dealt with at greater length, although an adequate treatment of it will have to wait for another occasion. All these theories, unless they take precautions, will appear to have consequences which run counter to the intuitions of the ordinary man. Nagel is the latest of many thinkers to try to take advantage of this apparent weakness in utilitarianism and related theories. It is easy for him to think up cases in which a utilitarian calculation would seem to justify actions contrary to principles which most of us, at least when we are not philosophizing, hold sacred. On careful inspection it will turn out that these cases are either fictitious or at least highly unusual, or else that the utilitarian calculations are very sketchily done, leaving out considerations which in practice would be most important. Nagel himself refers to "the abyss of utilitarian apologetics," and a utilitarian can readily admit that it is possible by a too superficial or facile application of utilitarian arguments to justify courses of action which a more thoroughgoing utilitarianism would condemn. But all the same, many have been put off utilitarianism by this move, which takes a good deal of methodological sophistication to counter.

Brandt, with his "two-level" approach, has given a clear indication of the way in which a utilitarian can defend himself against this attack. I wish, however, to set this defense within a more general framework of ethical theory, without claiming that Brandt would agree with all that I say. The "sacred principles" of the ordinary man, and the rules of war which are a crude attempt to apply them to a particular practical sphere, have an established place in any complete utilitarian theory; unfortunately utilitarians have not sufficiently emphasized this, and therefore "absolutists" have some excuse for ignor-

7. See the end of my paper in *Jowett Papers, 1968-1969*, ed. B. Y. Khanbhai et al. (Oxford, 1970), pp. 44-52.

ing it. Confusion has resulted on both sides from a failure to make clear what this established place is. The best *name* for it is that chosen by the deontologist Ross: "prima facie." Indeed, it would have been better for Nagel to use, to describe the view which he expounds, the old name "deontologist," instead of adopting the term "absolutist," which invites confusion with the kind of absolutist who is the opponent of relativism (whatever that may be). I trust that Nagel does not think that his utilitarian opponents are relativists. But although "prima facie" is a good name for these principles, it does not do much to explain their nature.

The defect in most deontological theories (and this would seem to apply to Ross, Anscombe, and Nagel) is that they have no coherent rational account to give of any level of moral thought above that of the man who knows some good simple moral principles and sticks to them. He is a very admirable person; and to question his principles (at any rate in situations of stress and temptation) is indeed to "show a corrupt mind."[8] But if philosophers do no more thinking than he is capable of, they will be able to give no account, either of how we are to come by these admirable principles, or of what we are to do when they conflict.

To achieve such an account, we have to adopt a "two-level" approach.[9] We have, that is to say, to recognize that the simple principles of the deontologist, important as they are, have their place at the level of character-formation (moral education and self-education). They are what we should be trying to inculcate into ourselves and our children if we want to stand the best chance, amid the stresses and temptations of the moral life, of doing what is for the best. Moore (who was a utilitarian) perhaps exaggerates when he says that we should *never* break principles which we know to be in general sound;[10] but a utilitarian who takes his utilitarianism seriously is likely to recommend that we form in ourselves, and continue in all our actions to foster, a firm disposition to abide by the principles whose general inculcation will have, all in all, the best consequences.

8. This phrase is used in a slightly different context by Professor G.E.M. Anscombe, "Modern Moral Philosophy," *Philosophy* 33, no. 124 (1958): 17 (reprinted in *The Is/Ought Question*, ed. W. D. Hudson [New York, 1970], p. 192).

9. See *Freedom and Reason*, pp. 42-44.

10. *Principia Ethica* (Cambridge, Eng., 1903), pp. 162ff.

The inculcation of these general principles has always been a prime concern of churches and other moral "authorities"; but in the present context it is more relevant to point out that this is equally true of armies. In the case of the typical military virtues this is obvious. Courage in attack and stubbornness in defense are strenuously cultivated; and the duty to obey orders and not to run away in battle is the center of all military training. These are not moral duties in the narrow sense (though their cultivation is instrumental to the performance of our moral duty when we are fighting in just wars, if any). If armies were to say to soldiers when training them, "On the battlefield, always do what is most conducive to the general good of mankind," or even "of your countrymen," nearly all the soldiers would easily convince themselves (battles being what they are) that the course most conducive to these desirable ends was headlong flight. Instead they say, "Leave those calculations to your superiors; they are probably in some bunker somewhere out of immediate personal danger, and therefore can consider more rationally and dispassionately, and with better information than you have, the question of whether to withdraw. Your job is to get on with the fighting." Only in this way can wars be won; and *if* the wars are just, the training was for the best. It is beyond the scope of this paper to discuss whether there are any just wars; I am inclined to think that there have been such in the past, though whether there could be just wars under modern conditions (except perhaps minor ones) is a hard question into which I shall not enter.[11]

The same is true of the more narrowly moral virtues. Let us assume for the sake of argument that it is for the greatest good that marital fidelity should be generally practiced. I could produce good arguments, concerned especially with the welfare of children, to show that this is so; but this is not the place for them. To say this is consistent with admitting that there may be cases in which adultery would be for the greatest good—for I said "generally" and not "universally." But fidelity will not be even generally practiced if people who are contemplating adultery ask themselves on each occasion whether their own might not be one of these cases; they will persuade themselves all too often that it is, when it is not. It is for the greatest good that statesmen

11. See my lecture "Peace," in *Applications of Moral Philosophy.*

should in general not tell lies in their public utterances—we have recently had an example of the troubles that ensue when they do, and Suez was another. It is true, admittedly, that situations can arise (say, when a currency is in trouble) in which it is quite obvious to a statesman that he ought to tell a lie; and this sort of thing can happen in private life too (which is why the ordinary man does not, for the most part, accept the duty of truthtelling as one without exceptions). But if statesmen and other men too do not cultivate the firm disposition to tell the truth and to hate lying, they will, both in this failure itself and in their particular acts, be most probably not acting for the best.

For the same reasons, as Brandt has indicated, military training should (and in all civilized armies does) include instruction in the laws and usages of war; and this training should be backed up by legal enforcement where possible. It looks as if the failure adequately to do this, and not any particular massacres and atrocities, ought to be the main target of critics of the United States Army in the present war (though it must be said in fairness that wars against guerrillas present peculiarly difficult problems). Even when armies are fighting wars which can be morally justified (if any), the individual soldier ought to be enabled to have as clear an idea of what he can legitimately do to the enemy as he has of when he can legitimately turn his back on the enemy. Neither kind of instruction is easy, but both are possible.

THE crucial question remains of what principles are to be the basis of this training. Brandt has sketched in a most illuminating way the kind of method by which this can be rationally determined; it amounts to an application of the five methods of moral reasoning which I was trying to merge at the beginning of this paper. He has also reached some provisional conclusions by this method; with these in the main I agree, though much more discussion is obviously needed.

A stumbling block to the understanding of the method may possibly be removed if I point out that there are in play here, in different parts of the reasoning, two quite distinct things which might both be called rule-utilitarianism. The failure to distinguish between them, and to see that they are quite compatible with each other provided that their spheres are kept separate, has caused havoc in this part of moral philosophy. There is first of all what may be called *general* rule-utilitarianism. This is the doctrine, supported in the last section, which says that we ought to inculcate and foster in ourselves and others, and in our actions cleave to, general principles whose cultivation is for the greatest good. In terms of a distinction which has been used in discussions of this subject, the utility appealed to by general rule-utilitarianism is an *acceptance*-utility—i.e., the utility of the general acceptance of certain principles, even if it falls short of universal observance. Such an insistence on having good general, fairly simple, teachable principles is essential to any view which takes the task of moral education (including self-education) seriously.

Secondly, there is what I have called *specific* rule-utilitarianism, one of the five mergeable theories which I listed at the beginning. This provides a kind of microscope wherewith we can, when we are in doubt about the general principles, examine particular cases in as minute specificity as we require, though always ending up with universal judgments, however specific. When using specific rule-utilitarianism we judge the morality of a particular act by assessing the utility of universal *observance* of the highly specific principle which requires acts of just this sort in just this sort of circumstances. By thus assessing particular acts in terms of the *observance*-utility of the highly specific universal principles enjoining them, we can assess the *acceptance*-utility of the general principles to be used in moral education. Once general principles are questioned, they can only be examined thus in the light of the particular results of their general adoption (of whether the policy of inculcating these principles is conducive *in general* to actions which can be thus minutely justified). Specific rule-utilitarianism thus has its place in higher-level discussions as to what the "good general principles" ought to be, and what should be done in cases where they conflict, or where there is a strong indication that the situation is so peculiar that the application of the general principle is unlikely to be for the best.

How are we to decide which cases these are? This is a matter for practical judgment rather than for theoretical reasoning (for the question is "Ought we to reason theoretically? Have we time? Are we likely to indulge in special pleading if we do?"). It might be objected to what I have said that although I have in theory allotted separate spheres to these two kinds of utilitarian reasoning, so that in principle they do not conflict, I have failed to say how we are to determine into which sphere any particular piece of reasoning is to fall. But the objection is not a real one. When faced with a choice between sticking to one of the simple general principles we have learnt and engaging in more specific reasoning, we have to ask ourselves which procedure is likely to approximate to the result which would be achieved by a reasoner not hampered by our human frailties. On the one side, there is the danger that a too rigid adherence to the standard general principles will lead us to disregard special features of the situation which ought to make a difference to our appraisal of it. On the other side, there is the danger that, if we once allow ourselves to question the general principle, our lack of knowledge and our partiality to our own interests may distort our reasoning. Which of these dangers is likely to be greater in a particular case for a particular person is not a philosophical question, and it is therefore no objection to a philosophical position that it does not answer it. My own inclination, in the light of my assessment of my own limitations, is to think that the occasions on which I should be safe in departing from my firm general principles (which are not of *extreme* generality) are very rare.

It is worth pointing out that when, by the employment of specific rule-utilitarianism at the higher level, we are seeking to select the best general principles for our general rule-utilitarianism of the lower level, we ought to consider those cases which are likely to occur. The use of hypothetical examples in philosophy, even fanciful ones, is perfectly legitimate; but in this particular field it can lead us astray. For we are seeking to discover principles which will be the most reliable in cases which are likely to preponderate in our actual experience; it would be out of place, therefore, to base our selection of the principles on a consideration of fanciful cases.

My AIM has been to convince the reader that a sound theoretical foundation can in principle be provided for moral thinking about war, and that this foundation is available to Brandt and to those who seek to put his conclusions into practice. They are much more likely on this basis than on an "absolutist" one to secure an improvement in our present customs, either by new international conventions or simply by the preservation and spread of right attitudes in soldiers and their commanders and governments. A great deal has been achieved in the past along these lines (do Nagel and those who write like him about the present war ever read what the wars of earlier centuries were like?). Although the invention of new weapons brings with it new temptations, which are often succumbed to, especially by those who have a temporary monopoly of these weapons, it is not impossible to bring their use under control, provided that their potential users are willing to adopt rational procedures in discussing the matter with one another. This is asking a lot; but the history of such negotiations is not exclusively a history of failure. In World War II poison gas was not, after all, used, though many expected that it would be. In both the world wars the Red Cross was for the most part respected. Without some background of written or unwritten international convention, neither of these restraints might have been exercised; and the conventions owed more to rational thought than to emotion, even if the reasoning had more of prudence in it than of morality.

Against these modest gains, I do not think that Nagel has much to offer. He is trying to justify the very same kind of rules as Brandt has, in my view, succeeded in justifying. But whereas Brandt is able to fit these rules into a rational system which also provides means for their selection and justification, Nagel, who is confined to one level of moral thinking, predictably finds himself torn between utilitarian arguments and absolutist ones, and thinks that in difficult cases he may be in "a moral blind alley," in which "there is no honorable or moral course for a man to take, no course free of guilt and responsibility for evil." It is dangerous to talk like this, because many people will think that, if there is no way of escaping guilt, only the neurotic will worry about it.

Is "guilt," in any case, the most appropriate concept in terms of which to discuss these problems? A man with good moral principles will be very likely to *feel* guilty whatever he does in cases such as Nagel is speaking of. If he did not, he would not be such a good man. For a person, on the other hand, who is mainly concerned to avoid feelings of guilt, the best advice is to grow a thick skin. If he finds this impossible, a *pis aller* would be to get himself a set of not too exacting principles of an absolutist sort, and think that he has done all that is required of him if he has not broken any of them—no matter how disastrous the consequences of his actions for other people. Though Nagel is perfectly right in saying that it is incoherent to suggest that one might "sacrifice one's moral integrity justifiably, in the service of a sufficiently worthy end," it is not incoherent to suggest that one might so sacrifice one's peace of mind. And moral integrity and peace of mind are easily confused if one equates having sinned with having a sense of having sinned. If, say, we are theists and can convince ourselves that God has laid down some relatively simple rules and that by observing these we can keep ourselves unspotted and safe from hellfire, this may seem a good way of avoiding the agony of mind which comes, in difficult cases, from calculation of the consequences of alternative actions. This may explain the undoubted attractions of absolutism.

The real Nagel, to his credit, avoids this kind of pharisaism; for he remains enough of a utilitarian to see that the implications of consistent absolutism are unacceptable. That is how he gets into his "moral blind alley"; but there is an obvious way out of it: to treat the general principles of the absolutist as indispensable practical guides, but not as epistemologically sacrosanct, and to admit a level of thought at which they can be criticized, justified, or even on occasion rejected in their particular applications when conflicts arise or when a case is sufficiently out of the ordinary to call for special consideration.

BUT EVEN if there were not this defect in Nagel's absolutism—that of trying to give his principles a higher status than they can have, and thus locking them in irresoluble conflict, on the same level, with the utilitarian principle in which he also believes—it would be defective for another reason: indeterminacy. He attempts to systematize and justify his intuitions by subsuming them under a more general principle: "whatever one does to another person intentionally must be aimed at him as a subject, with the intention that he receive it as a subject. It should manifest an attitude to *him* rather than just to the situation, and he should be able to recognize it and identify himself as its object." It is difficult to think that a principle as vague and obscure as this could be of much use in practical dilemmas. One would be likely to find rival parties justifying opposite courses of action on the basis of this same principle. We have grown accustomed to moral philosophers telling us that we can ascertain our duties to other people by appeal to an a priori principle that we ought to treat people as people.[12] But Nagel's is an unexpected use of the method, which displays how accommodating it can be. He has done nothing to show that one could not treat people as people just as well by hating them as by loving them. The simplest way, in dealing with the enemy and his friends and relations, of "manifesting an attitude to *them*," would be to learn to hate them. Then we can manifest this attitude by any barbarity that takes our fancy, in the assurance that we are not doing what Nagel's principle forbids. This would seem as good a way as any of avoiding being "bureaucratic," and of securing the "maintenance of a direct interpersonal response to the people one deals with."

In the days before wars became even as humane as they *sometimes* are now, this was an almost universal attitude. Anyone who reads the Bible, or Herodotus and Thucydides, can find massacres of *already defeated* peoples accepted as normal; and Priam in the *Iliad*, when he describes the horrors that await him at the "kill," when Troy is sacked, does not imply that the actions of the victors will be wicked—only unpleasant.[13]

I have probably got Nagel all wrong. Brandt interprets him more charitably; and maybe all he is saying is that moral judgments have to to universalizable. That is to say, we are to think of those affected by our actions, including the enemy, as people like ourselves, and do to them only what is permitted by a set of universal principles that we are prepared to see adopted for cases in which we are at the receiving end.[14] If this is what he is saying, his position is not so very different from my own. The difference is that I would include more people in the class of those whose sufferings are relevant to our moral decisions (for example, in the Hiroshima case, those that will die if the war is not ended quickly, as well as those actually killed by the bombing). I cannot find in Nagel's argument any justification for leaving the former class out; but if they are included, this version of the method he advocates will join the list of mergeable positions set out at the beginning of this paper. Only further clarification will reveal whether our views can be reconciled in this way.

12. See *Freedom and Reason*, pp. 211-213.
13. *Iliad* 22. 6off.
14. See *Freedom and Reason*, esp. chap. 6.

MICHAEL WALZER

Political Action:
The Problem of Dirty Hands[1]

The preceding essays first appeared in *Philosophy & Public Affairs* as a symposium on the rules of war which was actually (or at least more importantly) a symposium on another topic.[2] The actual topic was whether or not a man can ever face, or ever has to face, a moral dilemma, a situation where he must choose between two courses of action both of which it would be wrong for him to undertake. Thomas Nagel worriedly suggested that this could happen and that it did happen whenever someone was forced to choose between upholding an important moral principle and avoiding some looming disaster.[3] R. B. Brandt argued that it could not possibly happen, for there were guidelines we might follow and calculations we might go through which would necessarily yield the conclusion that one or the other course of action was the right one to undertake in the circumstances (or that it did not matter which we undertook). R. M. Hare explained how it was

1. An earlier version of this paper was read at the annual meeting of the Conference for the Study of Political Thought in New York, April 1971. I am indebted to Charles Taylor, who served as commentator at that time and encouraged me to think that its arguments might be right.

2. *Philosophy & Public Affairs* 1, no. 2 (Winter 1972).

3. For Nagel's description of a possible "moral blind alley," see pp. 22-24. Bernard Williams has made a similar suggestion, though without quite acknowledging it as his own: "many people can recognize the thought that a certain course of action is, indeed, the best thing to do on the whole in the circumstances, but that doing it involves doing something wrong" (*Morality: An Introduction to Ethics* [New York, 1972], p. 93).

that someone might wrongly suppose that he was faced with a moral dilemma: sometimes, he suggested, the precepts and principles of an ordinary man, the products of his moral education, come into conflict with injunctions developed at a higher level of moral discourse. But this conflict is, or ought to be, resolved at the higher level; there is no real dilemma.

I am not sure that Hare's explanation is at all comforting, but the question is important even if no such explanation is possible, perhaps especially so if this is the case. The argument relates not only to the coherence and harmony of the moral universe, but also to the relative ease or difficulty—or impossibility—of living a moral life. It is not, therefore, merely a philosopher's question. If such a dilemma can arise, whether frequently or very rarely, any of us might one day face it. Indeed, many men have faced it, or think they have, especially men involved in political activity or war. The dilemma, exactly as Nagel describes it, is frequently discussed in the literature of political action—in novels and plays dealing with politics and in the work of theorists too.

In modern times the dilemma appears most often as the problem of "dirty hands," and it is typically stated by the Communist leader Hoerderer in Sartre's play of that name: "I have dirty hands right up to the elbows. I've plunged them in filth and blood. Do you think you can govern innocently?"[4] My own answer is no, I don't think I could govern innocently; nor do most of us believe that those who govern us are innocent—as I shall argue below—even the best of them. But this does not mean that it isn't possible to do the right thing while governing. It means that a particular act of government (in a political party or in the state) may be exactly the right thing to do in utilitarian terms and yet leave the man who does it guilty of a moral wrong. The innocent man, afterwards, is no longer innocent. If on the other hand he remains innocent, chooses, that is, the "absolutist" side of Nagel's dilemma, he not only fails to do the right thing (in utilitarian terms), he may also fail to measure up to the duties of his office (which imposes on him a considerable responsibility for consequences and outcomes). Most often, of course, political leaders accept the utilitarian

4. Jean-Paul Sartre, *Dirty Hands*, in *No Exit and Three Other Plays*, trans. Lionel Abel (New York, n.d.), p. 224.

calculation; they try to measure up. One might offer a number of sardonic comments on this fact, the most obvious being that by the calculations they usually make they demonstrate the great virtues of the "absolutist" position. Nevertheless, we would not want to be governed by men who consistently adopted that position.

The notion of dirty hands derives from an effort to refuse "absolutism" without denying the reality of the moral dilemma. Though this may appear to utilitarian philosophers to pile confusion upon confusion, I propose to take it very seriously. For the literature I shall examine is the work of serious and often wise men, and it reflects, though it may also have helped to shape, popular thinking about politics. It is important to pay attention to that too. I shall do so without assuming, as Hare suggests one might, that everyday moral and political discourse constitutes a distinct level of argument, where content is largely a matter of pedagogic expediency.[5] If popular views are resistant (as they are) to utilitarianism, there may be something to learn from that and not merely something to explain about it.

I

Let me begin, then, with a piece of conventional wisdom to the effect that politicians are a good deal worse, morally worse, than the rest of us (it is the wisdom of the rest of us). Without either endorsing it or pretending to disbelieve it, I am going to expound this convention. For it suggests that the dilemma of dirty hands is a central feature of political life, that it arises not merely as an occasional crisis in the career of this or that unlucky politician but systematically and frequently.

Why is the politician singled out? Isn't he like the other entrepreneurs in an open society, who hustle, lie, intrigue, wear masks, smile and are villains? He is not, no doubt for many reasons, three of which I need to consider. First of all, the politician claims to play a different part than other entrepreneurs. He doesn't merely cater to our interests; he acts on our behalf, even in our name. He has purposes in mind, causes and projects that require the support and redound to the bene-

---

5. See pp. 53-58, esp. p. 54: "the simple principles of the deontologist . . . have their place at the level of character-formation (moral education and self-education)."

fit, not of each of us individually, but of all of us together. He hustles, lies, and intrigues *for us*—or so he claims. Perhaps he is right, or at least sincere, but we suspect that he acts for himself also. Indeed, he cannot serve us without serving himself, for success brings him power and glory, the greatest rewards that men can win from their fellows. The competition for these two is fierce; the risks are often great, but the temptations are greater. We imagine ourselves succumbing. Why should our representatives act differently? Even if they would like to act differently, they probably can not: for other men are all too ready to hustle and lie for power and glory, and it is the others who set the terms of the competition. Hustling and lying are necessary because power and glory are so desirable—that is, so widely desired. And so the men who act for us and in our name are necessarily hustlers and liars.

Politicians are also thought to be worse than the rest of us because they rule over us, and the pleasures of ruling are much greater than the pleasures of being ruled. The successful politician becomes the visible architect of our restraint. He taxes us, licenses us, forbids and permits us, directs us to this or that distant goal—all for our greater good. Moreover, he takes chances for our greater good that put us, or some of us, in danger. Sometimes he puts himself in danger too, but politics, after all, is his adventure. It is not always ours. There are undoubtedly times when it is good or necessary to direct the affairs of other people and to put them in danger. But we are a little frightened of the man who seeks, ordinarily and every day, the power to do so. And the fear is reasonable enough. The politician has, or pretends to have, a kind of confidence in his own judgment that the rest of us know to be presumptuous in any man.

The presumption is especially great because the victorious politician uses violence and the threat of violence—not only against foreign nations in our defense but also against us, and again ostensibly for our greater good. This is a point emphasized and perhaps overemphasized by Max Weber in his essay "Politics as a Vocation."[6] It has not, so far as I can tell, played an overt or obvious part in the development of the convention I am examining. The stock figure is the lying, not the murderous, politician—though the murderer lurks in the background,

6. In *From Max Weber: Essays in Sociology*, trans. and ed. Hans H. Gerth and C. Wright Mills (New York, 1946), pp. 77-128.

appearing most often in the form of the revolutionary or terrorist, very rarely as an ordinary magistrate or official. Nevertheless, the sheer weight of official violence in human history does suggest the kind of power to which politicians aspire, the kind of power they want to wield, and it may point to the roots of our half-conscious dislike and unease. The men who act for us and in our name are often killers, or seem to become killers too quickly and too easily.

Knowing all this or most of it, good and decent people still enter political life, aiming at some specific reform or seeking a general reformation. They are then required to learn the lesson Machiavelli first set out to teach: "how not to be good."[7] Some of them are incapable of learning; many more profess to be incapable. But they will not succeed unless they learn, for they have joined the terrible competition for power and glory; they have chosen to work and struggle as Machiavelli says, among "so many who are not good." They can do no good themselves unless they win the struggle, which they are unlikely to do unless they are willing and able to use the necessary means. So we are suspicious even of the best of winners. It is not a sign of our perversity if we think them only more clever than the rest. They have not won, after all, because they were good, or not only because of that, but also because they were not good. No one succeeds in politics without getting his hands dirty. This is conventional wisdom again, and again I don't mean to insist that it is true without qualification. I repeat it only to disclose the moral dilemma inherent in the convention. For sometimes it is right to try to succeed, and then it must also be right to get one's hands dirty. But one's hands get dirty from doing what it is wrong to do. And how can it be wrong to do what is right? Or, how can we get our hands dirty by doing what we ought to do?

II

It will be best to turn quickly to some examples. I have chosen two, one relating to the struggle for power and one to its exercise. I should stress that in both these cases the men who face the dilemma of dirty hands have in an important sense chosen to do so; the cases tell us

7. See *The Prince*, chap. XV; cf. *The Discourses*, bk. I, chaps. IX and XVIII. I quote from the Modern Library edition of the two works (New York, 1950), p. 57.

nothing about what it would be like, so to speak, to fall into the dilemma; nor shall I say anything about that here. Politicians often argue that they have no right to keep their hands clean, and that may well be true of them, but it is not so clearly true of the rest of us. Probably we do have a right to avoid, if we possibly can, those positions in which we might be forced to do terrible things. This might be regarded as the moral equivalent of our legal right not to incriminate ourselves. Good men will be in no hurry to surrender it, though there are reasons for doing so sometimes, and among these are or might be the reasons good men have for entering politics. But let us imagine a politician who does not agree to that: he wants to do good only by doing good, or at least he is certain that he can stop short of the most corrupting and brutal uses of political power. Very quickly that certainty is tested. What do we think of him then?

He wants to win the election, someone says, but he doesn't want to get his hands dirty. This is meant as a disparagement, even though it also means that the man being criticized is the sort of man who will not lie, cheat, bargain behind the backs of his supporters, shout absurdities at public meetings, or manipulate other men and women. Assuming that this particular election ought to be won, it is clear, I think, that the disparagement is justified. If the candidate didn't want to get his hands dirty, he should have stayed at home; if he can't stand the heat, he should get out of the kitchen, and so on. His decision to run was a commitment (to all of us who think the election important) to try to win, that is, to do within rational limits whatever is necessary to win. But the candidate is a moral man. He has principles and a history of adherence to those principles. That is why we are supporting him. Perhaps when he refuses to dirty his hands, he is simply insisting on being the sort of man he is. And isn't that the sort of man we want?

Let us look more closely at this case. In order to win the election the candidate must make a deal with a dishonest ward boss, involving the granting of contracts for school construction over the next four years. Should he make the deal? Well, at least he shouldn't be surprised by the offer, most of us would probably say (a conventional piece of sarcasm). And he should accept it or not, depending on exactly what is at stake in the election. But that is not the candidate's view. He is extremely reluctant even to consider the deal, puts off his aides when they remind him of it, refuses to calculate its possible effects upon the campaign. Now, if he is acting this way because the very thought of bargaining with that particular ward boss makes him feel unclean, his reluctance isn't very interesting. His feelings by themselves are not important. But he may also have reasons for his reluctance. He may know, for example, that some of his supporters support him precisely because they believe he is a good man, and this means to them a man who won't make such deals. Or he may doubt his own motives for considering the deal, wondering whether it is the political campaign or his own candidacy that makes the bargain at all tempting. Or he may believe that if he makes deals of this sort now he may not be able later on to achieve those ends that make the campaign worthwhile, and he may not feel entitled to take such risks with a future that is not only his own future. Or he may simply think that the deal is dishonest and therefore wrong, corrupting not only himself but all those human relations in which he is involved.

Because he has scruples of this sort, we know him to be a good man. But we view the campaign in a certain light, estimate its importance in a certain way, and hope that he will overcome his scruples and make the deal. It is important to stress that we don't want just *anyone* to make the deal; we want *him* to make it, precisely because he has scruples about it. We know he is doing right when he makes the deal because he knows he is doing wrong. I don't mean merely that he will feel badly or even very badly after he makes the deal. If he is the good man I am imagining him to be, he will feel guilty, that is, he will believe himself to be guilty. That is what it means to have dirty hands.

All this may become clearer if we look at a more dramatic example, for we are, perhaps, a little blasé about political deals and disinclined to worry much about the man who makes one. So consider a politician who has seized upon a national crisis—a prolonged colonial war—to reach for power. He and his friends win office pledged to decolonization and peace; they are honestly committed to both, though not without some sense of the advantages of the commitment. In any case, they have no responsibility for the war; they have steadfastly opposed it. Immediately, the politician goes off to the colonial capital to open negotiations with the rebels. But the capital is in the grip of a terrorist campaign, and the first decision the new leader faces is this: he is asked to authorize the torture of a captured rebel leader who knows or probably knows the location of a number of bombs hidden in apartment buildings around the city, set to go off within the next twenty-four hours. He orders the man tortured, convinced that he must do so for the sake of the people who might otherwise die in the explosions— even though he believes that torture is wrong, indeed abominable, not just sometimes, but always.[8] He had expressed this belief often and angrily during his own campaign; the rest of us took it as a sign of his goodness. How should we regard him now? (How should he regard himself?)

Once again, it does not seem enough to say that he should feel very badly. But why not? Why shouldn't he have feelings like those of St. Augustine's melancholy soldier, who understood both that his war was just and that killing, even in a just war, is a terrible thing to do?[9] The difference is that Augustine did not believe that it was wrong to kill in a just war; it was just sad, or the sort of thing a good man would be saddened by. But he might have thought it wrong to torture in a just war, and later Catholic theorists have certainly thought it wrong. Moreover, the politician I am imagining thinks it wrong, as do many of us who supported him. Surely we have a right to expect more than melancholy from him now. When he ordered the prisoner tortured, he committed a moral crime and he accepted a moral burden. Now he is a guilty man. His willingness to acknowledge and bear (and perhaps to repent and do penance for) his guilt is evidence, and it is the only evidence he can offer us, both that he

8. I leave aside the question of whether the prisoner is himself responsible for the terrorist campaign. Perhaps he opposed it in meetings of the rebel organization. In any case, whether he deserves to be punished or not, he does not deserve to be tortured.

9. Other writers argued that Christians must never kill, even in a just war; and there was also an intermediate position which suggests the origins of the idea of dirty hands. Thus Basil The Great (Bishop of Caesarea in the fourth century A.D.): "Killing in war was differentiated by our fathers from murder . . . nevertheless, perhaps it would be well that those whose hands are unclean abstain from communion for three years." Here dirty hands are a kind of impurity or unworthiness, which is not the same as guilt, though closely related to it. For a general survey of these and other Christian views, see Roland H. Bainton, *Christian Attitudes Toward War and Peace* (New York, 1960), esp. chaps. 5-7.

is not too good for politics and that he is good enough. Here is the moral politician: it is by his dirty hands that we know him. If he were a moral man and nothing else, his hands would not be dirty; if he were a politician and nothing else, he would pretend that they were clean.

III

Machiavelli's argument about the need to learn how not to be good clearly implies that there are acts known to be bad quite apart from the immediate circumstances in which they are performed or not performed. He points to a distinct set of political methods and strategems which good men must study (by reading his books), not only because their use does not come naturally, but also because they are explicitly condemned by the moral teachings good men accept—and whose acceptance serves in turn to mark men as good. These methods may be condemned because they are thought contrary to divine law or to the order of nature or to our moral sense, or because in prescribing the law to ourselves we have individually or collectively prohibited them. Machiavelli does not commit himself on such issues, and I shall not do so either if I can avoid it. The effects of these different views are, at least in one crucial sense, the same. They take out of our hands the constant business of attaching moral labels to such Machiavellian methods as deceit and betrayal. Such methods are simply bad. They are the sort of thing that good men avoid, at least until they have learned how not to be good.

Now, if there is no such class of actions, there is no dilemma of dirty hands, and the Machiavellian teaching loses what Machiavelli surely intended it to have, its disturbing and paradoxical character. He can then be understood to be saying that political actors must sometimes overcome their moral inhibitions, but not that they must sometimes commit crimes. I take it that utilitarian philosophers also want to make the first of these statements and to deny the second. From their point of view, the candidate who makes a corrupt deal and the official who authorizes the torture of a prisoner must be described as good men (given the cases as I have specified them), who ought, perhaps, to be honored for making the right decision when it was a hard decision to make. There are three ways of developing this argument.

First, it might be said that every political choice ought to be made solely in terms of its particular and immediate circumstances—in terms, that is, of the reasonable alternatives, available knowledge, likely consequences, and so on. Then the good man will face difficult choices (when his knowledge of options and outcomes is radically uncertain), but it cannot happen that he will face a moral dilemma. Indeed, if he always makes decisions in this way, and has been taught from childhood to do so, he will never have to overcome his inhibitions, whatever he does, for how could he have acquired inhibitions? Assuming further that he weighs the alternatives and calculates the consequences seriously and in good faith, he cannot commit a crime, though he can certainly make a mistake, even a very serious mistake. Even when he lies and tortures, his hands will be clean, for he has done what he should do as best he can, standing alone in a moment of time, forced to choose.

This is in some ways an attractive description of moral decision-making, but it is also a very improbable one. For while any one of us may stand alone, and so on, when we make this or that decision, we are not isolated or solitary in our moral lives. Moral life is a social phenomenon, and it is constituted at least in part by rules, the knowing of which (and perhaps the making of which) we share with our fellows. The experience of coming up against these rules, challenging their prohibitions, and explaining ourselves to other men and women is so common and so obviously important that no account of moral decision-making can possibly fail to come to grips with it. Hence the second utilitarian argument: such rules do indeed exist, but they are not really prohibitions of wrongful actions (though they do, perhaps for pedagogic reasons, have that form). They are moral guidelines, summaries of previous calculations. They ease our choices in ordinary cases, for we can simply follow their injunctions and do what has been found useful in the past; in exceptional cases they serve as signals warning us against doing too quickly or without the most careful calculations what has not been found useful in the past. But they do no more than that; they have no other purpose, and so it cannot be the case that it is or even might be a crime to override them.[10] Nor is it

10. Brandt's rules do not appear to be of the sort that can be overridden—except perhaps by a soldier who decides that he just *won't* kill any more civil-

necessary to feel guilty when one does so. Once again, if it is right
to break the rule in some hard case, after conscientiously worrying
about it, the man who acts (especially if he knows that many of his
fellows would simply worry rather than act) may properly feel pride
in his achievement.

But this view, it seems to me, captures the reality of our moral life
no better than the last. It may well be right to say that moral rules
ought to have the character of guidelines, but it seems that in fact
they do not. Or at least, we defend ourselves when we break the rules
as if they had some status entirely independent of their previous utility (and we rarely feel proud of ourselves). The defenses we normally
offer are not simply justifications; they are also excuses. Now, as
Austin says, these two can *seem* to come very close together—indeed,
I shall suggest that they can appear side by side in the same sentence
—but they are conceptually distinct, differentiated in this crucial respect: an excuse is typically an admission of fault; a justification is
typically a denial of fault and an assertion of innocence.[11] Consider
a well-known defense from Shakespeare's *Hamlet* that has often re-
appeared in political literature: "I must be cruel only to be kind."[12]
The words are spoken on an occasion when Hamlet is actually being
cruel to his mother. I will leave aside the possibility that she deserves
to hear (to be forced to listen to) every harsh word he utters, for
Hamlet himself makes no such claim—and if she did indeed deserve
that, his words might not be cruel or he might not be cruel for speaking them. "I must be cruel" contains the excuse, since it both admits a
fault and suggests that Hamlet has no choice but to commit it. He is
doing what he has to do; he can't help himself (given the ghost's
command, the rotten state of Denmark, and so on). The rest of the
sentence is a justification, for it suggests that Hamlet intends and ex-
pects kindness to be the outcome of his actions—we must assume that

---

ians, no matter what cause is served—since all they require is careful calculation.
But I take it that rules of a different sort, which have the form of ordinary injunctions and prohibitions, can and often do figure in what is called "rule-utilitarianism."

11. J. L. Austin, "A Plea for Excuses," in *Philosophical Papers*, ed. J. O.
Urmson and G. J. Warnock (Oxford, 1961), pp. 123-152.

12. *Hamlet* 3.4.178.

he means greater kindness, kindness to the right persons, or some such. It is not, however, so complete a justification that Hamlet is able to say that he is not *really* being cruel. "Cruel" and "kind" have exactly the same status; they both follow the verb "to be," and so they perfectly reveal the moral dilemma.[13]

When rules are overridden, we do not talk or act as if they had been set aside, canceled, or annulled. They still stand and have this much effect at least: that we know we have done something wrong even if what we have done was also the best thing to do on the whole in the circumstances.[14] Or at least we feel that way, and this feeling is itself a crucial feature of our moral life. Hence the third utilitarian argument, which recognizes the usefulness of guilt and seeks to explain it. There are, it appears, good reasons for "overvaluing" as well as for overriding the rules. For the consequences might be very bad indeed if the rules were overridden every time the moral calculation seemed to go against them. It is probably best if most men do not calculate too nicely, but simply follow the rules; they are less likely to make mistakes that way, all in all. And so a good man (or at least an ordinary good man) will respect the rules rather more than he would if he thought them merely guidelines, and he will feel guilty when he overrides them. Indeed, if he did not feel guilty, "he would not be such a good man."[15] It is by his feelings that we know him. Because of those feelings he will never be in a hurry to override the rules, but will wait until there is no choice, acting only to avoid consequences that are both imminent and almost certainly disastrous.

The obvious difficulty with this argument is that the feeling whose usefulness is being explained is most unlikely to be felt by someone who is convinced only of its usefulness. He breaks a utilitarian rule (guideline), let us say, for good utilitarian reasons: but can he then

13. Compare the following lines from Bertold Brecht's poem "To Posterity": "Alas, we/ Who wished to lay the foundations of kindness/ Could not ourselves be kind . . ." (*Selected Poems*, trans. H. R. Hays [New York, 1969], p. 177). This is more of an excuse, less of a justification (the poem is an *apologia*).

14. Robert Nozick discusses some of the possible effects of overriding a rule in his "Moral Complications and Moral Structures," *Natural Law Forum* 13 (1968): 34-35 and notes. Nozick suggests that what may remain after one has broken a rule (for good reasons) is a "duty to make reparations." He does not call this "guilt," though the two notions are closely connected.

15. Hare, p. 59.

feel guilty, also for good utilitarian reasons, when he has no reason for believing that he *is* guilty? Imagine a moral philosopher expounding the third argument to a man who actually does feel guilty or to the sort of man who is likely to feel guilty. Either the man won't accept the utilitarian explanation as an account of his feeling about the rules (probably the best outcome from a utilitarian point of view) or he will accept it and then cease to feel that (useful) feeling. But I do not want to exclude the possibility of a kind of superstitious anxiety, the possibility, that is, that some men will continue to feel guilty even after they have been taught, and have agreed, that they cannot possibly *be* guilty. It is best to say only that the more fully they accept the utilitarian account, the less likely they are to feel that (useful) feeling. The utilitarian account is not at all useful, then, if political actors accept it, and that may help us to understand why it plays, as Hare has pointed out, so small a part in our moral education.[16]

16. There is another possible utilitarian position, suggested in Maurice Merleau-Ponty's *Humanism and Terror*, trans. John O'Neill (Boston, 1970). According to this view, the agony and the guilt feelings experienced by the man who makes a "dirty hands" decision derive from his radical uncertainty about the actual outcome. Perhaps the awful thing he is doing will be done in vain; the results he hopes for won't occur; the only outcome will be the pain he has caused or the deceit he has fostered. Then (and only then) he will indeed have committed a crime. On the other hand, if the expected good does come, then (and only then) he can abandon his guilt feelings; he can say, and the rest of us must agree, that he is justified. This is a kind of delayed utilitarianism, where justification is a matter of actual and not at all of predicted outcomes. It is not implausible to imagine a political actor anxiously awaiting the "verdict of history." But suppose the verdict is in his favor (assuming that there is a *final* verdict or a statute of limitations on possible verdicts): he will surely feel relieved—more so, no doubt, than the rest of us. I can see no reason, however, why he should think himself justified, if he is a good man and knows that what he did was wrong. Perhaps the victims of his crime, seeing the happy result, will absolve him, but history has no powers of absolution. Indeed, history is more likely to play tricks on our moral judgment. Predicted outcomes are at least thought to follow from our own acts (this is the prediction), but actual outcomes almost certainly have a multitude of causes, the combination of which may well be fortuitous. Merleau-Ponty stresses the risks of political decision-making so heavily that he turns politics into a gamble with time and circumstance. But the anxiety of the gambler is of no great moral interest. Nor is it much of a barrier, as Merleau-Ponty's book makes all too clear, to the commission of the most terrible crimes.

IV

One further comment on the third argument: it is worth stressing that to feel guilty is to suffer, and that the men whose guilt feelings are here called useful are themselves innocent according to the utilitarian account. So we seem to have come upon another case where the suffering of the innocent is permitted and even encouraged by utilitarian calculation.[17] But surely an innocent man who has done something painful or hard (but justified) should be helped to avoid or escape the sense of guilt; he might reasonably expect the assistance of his fellow men, even of moral philosophers, at such a time. On the other hand, if we intuitively think it true of some other man that he *should* feel guilty, then we ought to be able to specify the nature of his guilt (and if he is a good man, win his agreement). I think I can construct a case which, with only small variation, highlights what is different in these two situations.

Consider the common practice of distributing rifles loaded with blanks to some of the members of a firing squad. The individual men are not told whether their own weapons are lethal, and so though all of them look like executioners to the victim in front of them, none of them know whether they are really executioners or not. The purpose of this stratagem is to relieve each man of the sense that he is a killer. It can hardly relieve him of whatever moral responsibility he incurs by serving on a firing squad, and that is not its purpose, for the execution is not thought to be (and let us grant this to be the case) an immoral or wrongful act. But the inhibition against killing another human being is so strong that even if the men believe that what they are doing is right, they will still feel guilty. Uncertainty as to their actual role apparently reduces the intensity of these feelings. If this is so, the stratagem is perfectly justifiable, and one can only rejoice in every case where it succeeds—for every success subtracts one from the number of innocent men who suffer.

But we would feel differently, I think, if we imagine a man who believes (and let us assume here that we believe also) either that capital

17. Cf. the cases suggested by David Ross, *The Right and the Good* (Oxford, 1930), pp. 56-57, and E. F. Carritt, *Ethical and Political Thinking* (Oxford, 1947), p. 65.

punishment is wrong or that this particular victim is innocent, but who nevertheless agrees to participate in the firing squad for some overriding political or moral reason—I won't try to suggest what that reason might be. If he is comforted by the trick with the rifles, then we can be reasonably certain that his opposition to capital punishment or his belief in the victim's innocence is not morally serious. And if it is serious, he will not merely feel guilty, he will know that he is guilty (and we will know it too), though he may also believe (and we may agree) that he has good reasons for incurring the guilt. Our guilt feelings can be tricked away when they are isolated from our moral beliefs, as in the first case, but not when they are allied with them, as in the second. The beliefs themselves and the rules which are believed in can only be *overridden*, a painful process which forces a man to weigh the wrong he is willing to do in order to do right, and which leaves pain behind, and should do so, even after the decision has been made.

v

That is the dilemma of dirty hands as it has been experienced by political actors and written about in the literature of political action. I don't want to argue that it is only a political dilemma. No doubt we can get our hands dirty in private life also, and sometimes, no doubt, we should. But the issue is posed most dramatically in politics for the three reasons that make political life the kind of life it is, because we claim to act for others but also serve ourselves, rule over others, and use violence against them. It is easy to get one's hands dirty in politics and it is often right to do so. But it is not easy to teach a good man how not to be good, nor is it easy to explain such a man to himself once he has committed whatever crimes are required of him. At least, it is not easy once we have agreed to use the word "crimes" and to live with (because we have no choice) the dilemma of dirty hands. Still, the agreement is common enough, and on its basis there have developed three broad traditions of explanation, three ways of thinking about dirty hands, which derive in some very general fashion from neoclassical, Protestant, and Catholic perspectives on politics and morality. I want to try to say something very briefly about each of them, or rather about a representative example of each of them, for each seems to me partly right. But I don't think I can put together the compound view that might be wholly right.

The first tradition is best represented by Machiavelli, the first man, so far as I know, to state the paradox that I am examining. The good man who aims to found or reform a republic must, Machiavelli tells us, do terrible things to reach his goal. Like Romulus, he must murder his brother; like Numa, he must lie to the people. Sometimes, however, "when the act accuses, the result excuses."[18] This sentence from *The Discourses* is often taken to mean that the politician's deceit and cruelty are justified by the good results he brings about. But if they were justified, it wouldn't be necessary to learn what Machiavelli claims to teach: how not to be good. It would only be necessary to learn how to be good in a new, more difficult, perhaps roundabout way. That is not Machiavelli's argument. His political judgments are indeed consequentialist in character, but not his moral judgments. We know whether cruelty is used well or badly by its effects over time. But that it is bad to use cruelty we know in some other way. The deceitful and cruel politician is excused (if he succeeds) only in the sense that the rest of us come to agree that the results were "worth it" or, more likely, that we simply forget his crimes when we praise his success.

It is important to stress Machiavelli's own commitment to the existence of moral standards. His paradox depends upon that commitment as it depends upon the general stability of the standards—which he upholds in his consistent use of words like good and bad.[19] If he wants the standards to be disregarded by good men more often than they are, he has nothing with which to replace them and no other way of recognizing the good men except by their allegiance to those same standards. It is exceedingly rare, he writes, that a good man is willing to employ bad means to become prince.[20] Machiavelli's purpose is to persuade such a person to make the attempt, and he holds out the supreme political rewards, power and glory, to the man who does so and succeeds. The good man is not rewarded (or excused), how-

18. *The Discourses*, bk. I, chap. IX (p. 139).

19. For a very different view of Machiavelli, see Isaiah Berlin, "The Question of Machiavelli," *The New York Review of Books*, 4 November 1971.

20. *The Discourses*, bk. I, chap. XVIII (p. 171).

ever, merely for his willingness to get his hands dirty. He must do bad things well. There is no reward for doing bad things badly, though they are done with the best of intentions. And so political action necessarily involves taking a risk. But it should be clear that what is risked is not personal goodness—*that is thrown away*—but power and glory. If the politician succeeds, he is a hero; eternal praise is the supreme reward for not being good.

What the penalties are for not being good, Machiavelli doesn't say, and it is probably for this reason above all that his moral sensitivity has so often been questioned. He is suspect not because he tells political actors they must get their hands dirty, but because he does not specify the state of mind appropriate to a man with dirty hands. A Machiavellian hero has no inwardness. What he thinks of himself we don't know. I would guess, along with most other readers of Machiavelli, that he basks in his glory. But then it is difficult to account for the strength of his original reluctance to learn how not to be good. In any case, he is the sort of man who is unlikely to keep a diary and so we cannot find out what he thinks. Yet we do want to know; above all, we want a record of his anguish. That is a sign of our own conscientiousness and of the impact on us of the second tradition of thought that I want to examine, in which personal anguish sometimes seems the only acceptable excuse for political crimes.

The second tradition is best represented, I think, by Max Weber, who outlines its essential features with great power at the very end of his essay "Politics as a Vocation." For Weber, the good man with dirty hands is a hero still, but he is a tragic hero. In part, his tragedy is that though politics is his vocation, he has not been called by God and so cannot be justified by Him. Weber's hero is alone in a world that seems to belong to Satan, and his vocation is entirely his own choice. He still wants what Christian magistrates have always wanted, both to do good in the world and to save his soul, but now these two ends have come into sharp contradiction. They are contradictory because of the necessity for violence in a world where God has not instituted the sword. The politician takes the sword himself, and only by doing so does he measure up to his vocation. With full consciousness of what he is doing, he does bad in order to do good, and surrenders his soul. He "lets himself in," Weber says, "for the diabolic forces lurking in all violence." Perhaps Machiavelli also meant to suggest that his hero surrenders salvation in exchange for glory, but he does not explicitly say so. Weber is absolutely clear: "the genius or demon of politics lives in an inner tension with the god of love . . . [which] can at any time lead to an irreconcilable conflict."[21] His politician views this conflict when it comes with a tough realism, never pretends that it might be solved by compromise, chooses politics once again, and turns decisively away from love. Weber writes about this choice with a passionate high-mindedness that makes a concern for one's soul seem no more elevated than a concern for one's flesh. Yet the reader never doubts that his mature, superbly trained, relentless, objective, responsible, and disciplined political leader is also a suffering servant. His choices are hard and painful, and he pays the price not only while making them but forever after. A man doesn't lose his soul one day and find it the next.

The difficulties with this view will be clear to anyone who has ever met a suffering servant. Here is a man who lies, intrigues, sends other men to their death—and suffers. He does what he must do with a heavy heart. None of us can know, he tells us, how much it costs him to do his duty. Indeed, we cannot, for he himself fixes the price he pays. And that is the trouble with this view of political crime. We suspect the suffering servant of either masochism or hypocrisy or both, and while we are often wrong, we are not always wrong. Weber attempts to resolve the problem of dirty hands entirely within the confines of the individual conscience, but I am inclined to think that this is neither possible nor desirable. The self-awareness of the tragic hero is obviously of great value. We want the politician to have an inner life at least something like that which Weber describes. But sometimes the hero's suffering needs to be socially expressed (for like punishment, it confirms and reinforces our sense that certain acts are wrong). And equally important, it sometimes needs to be socially limited. We don't want to be ruled by men who have lost their souls.

21. "Politics as a Vocation," pp. 125-126. But sometimes a political leader does choose the "absolutist" side of the conflict, and Weber writes (p. 127) that it is "immensely moving when a *mature* man . . . aware of a responsibility for the consequences of his conduct . . . reaches a point where he says: 'Here I stand; I can do no other.'" Unfortunately, he does not suggest just where that point is or even where it might be.

A politician with dirty hands needs a soul, and it is best for us all if he has some hope of personal salvation, however that is conceived. It is not the case that when he does bad in order to do good he surrenders himself forever to the demon of politics. He commits a determinate crime, and he must pay a determinate penalty. When he has done so, his hands will be clean again, or as clean as human hands can ever be. So the Catholic Church has always taught, and this teaching is central to the third tradition that I want to examine.

Once again I will take a latter-day and a lapsed representative of the tradition and consider Albert Camus' *The Just Assassins*. The heroes of this play are terrorists at work in nineteenth-century Russia. The dirt on their hands is human blood. And yet Camus' admiration for them, he tells us, is complete. We consent to being criminals, one of them says, but there is nothing with which anyone can reproach us. Here is the dilemma of dirty hands in a new form. The heroes are innocent criminals, just assassins, because, having killed, they are prepared to die—*and will die*. Only their execution, by the same despotic authorities they are attacking, will complete the action in which they are engaged: dying, they need make no excuses. That is the end of their guilt and pain. The execution is not so much punishment as self-punishment and expiation. On the scaffold they wash their hands clean and, unlike the suffering servant, they die happy.

Now the argument of the play when presented in so radically simplified a form may seem a little bizarre, and perhaps it is marred by the moral extremism of Camus' politics. "Political action has limits," he says in a preface to the volume containing *The Just Assassins*, "and there is no good and just action but what recognizes those limits and if it must go beyond them, at least accepts death."[22] I am less interested here in the violence of that "at least"—what else does he have in mind?—than in the sensible doctrine that it exaggerates. That doctrine might best be described by an analogy: just assassination, I want to suggest, is like civil disobedience. In both men violate a set of rules, go beyond a moral or legal limit, in order to do what they believe they should do. At the same time, they acknowledge their responsibility for the violation by accepting punishment or doing penance. But

22. *Caligula and Three Other Plays* (New York, 1958), p. x. (The preface is translated by Justin O'Brian, the plays by Stuart Gilbert.)

there is also a difference between the two, which has to do with the difference between law and morality. In most cases of civil disobedience the laws of the state are broken for moral reasons, and the state provides the punishment. In most cases of dirty hands moral rules are broken for reasons of state, and no one provides the punishment. There is rarely a Czarist executioner waiting in the wings for politicians with dirty hands, even the most deserving among them. Moral rules are not usually enforced against the sort of actor I am considering, largely because he acts in an official capacity. If they were enforced, dirty hands would be no problem. We would simply honor the man who did bad in order to do good, and at the same time we would punish him. We would honor him for the good he has done, and we would punish him for the bad he has done. We would punish him, that is, for the same reasons we punish anyone else; it is not my purpose here to defend any particular view of punishment. In any case, there seems no way to establish or enforce the punishment. Short of the priest and the confessional, there are no authorities to whom we might entrust the task.

I am nevertheless inclined to think Camus' view the most attractive of the three, if only because it requires us at least to imagine a punishment or a penance that fits the crime and so to examine closely the nature of the crime. The others do not require that. Once he has launched his career, the crimes of Machiavelli's prince seem subject only to prudential control. And the crimes of Weber's tragic hero are limited only by *his* capacity for suffering and not, as they should be, by *our* capacity for suffering. In neither case is there any explicit reference back to the moral code, once it has, at great personal cost to be sure, been set aside. The question posed by Sartre's Hoerderer (whom I suspect of being a suffering servant) is rhetorical, and the answer is obvious (I have already given it), but the characteristic sweep of both is disturbing. Since it is concerned only with those crimes that ought to be committed, the dilemma of dirty hands seems to exclude questions of degree. Wanton or excessive cruelty is not at issue, any more than is cruelty directed at bad ends. But political action is so uncertain that politicians necessarily take moral as well as political risks, committing crimes that they only think ought to be committed. They override the rules without ever being certain that they have found the best way to the results they hope to achieve, and we don't want them to do that too quickly or too often. So it is important that the moral stakes be very high—which is to say, that the rules be rightly valued. That, I suppose, is the reason for Camus' extremism. Without the executioner, however, there is no one to set the stakes or maintain the values except ourselves, and probably no way to do either except through philosophic reiteration and political activity.

"We shall not abolish lying by refusing to tell lies," says Hoerderer, "but by using every means at hand to abolish social classes."[23] I suspect we shall not abolish lying at all, but we might see to it that fewer lies were told if we contrived to deny power and glory to the greatest liars—except, of course, in the case of those lucky few whose extraordinary achievements make us forget the lies they told. If Hoerderer succeeds in abolishing social classes, perhaps he will join the lucky few. Meanwhile, he lies, manipulates, and kills, and we must make sure he pays the price. We won't be able to do that, however, without getting our own hands dirty, and then we must find some way of paying the price ourselves.

23. *Dirty Hands*, p. 223.

War and Moral Responsibility

PART II

MICHAEL WALZER

World War II:
Why Was This War Different?

I

The war against Nazi Germany is an extreme case, but not—one meets young men and women who need to be told—an imaginary case. It happened, and the event (and Nazism itself) has properly been the focus of much of our political and sociological theorizing in the years since. It has not figured largely, however, in our speculations about the just war, for reasons that I hope will become apparent as I write. Revived by the atomic threat and then by the war in Vietnam, American interest in just war theory has been marked, like much else in contemporary thought, by a disbelief in history. The fall of man, it sometimes appears, took place at Hiroshima.[1] There are occasional retrospective glances at Nazi aggression or, more often, at such Allied outrages as the firebombing of Dresden. But these call forth easy judgments, which rarely engage the human experience of those years. I don't mean that they fail to speak to the suffering caused by the Nazis and by the Allied war against them; they miss the fearfulness, the sense of danger, the ultimate character of the struggle.

Most wars are described in ultimate terms while they are being fought. Soldiers are encouraged, presumably, if they believe that the stakes are high, that freedom, justice, civilization itself are threatened.

This is a revised version of a paper originally presented at the annual meeting of the American Political Science Association, 8-12 September 1970.

1. Much of the literature on the just war continues to be the work of Christian theologians, who, unless they are very up-to-date, know perfectly well when the fall occurred. I am referring rather to a new way of talking about war, pervasive especially at our universities.

To the historian, or to the detached bystander, these descriptions are rarely plausible. The course of European history might well have been different, for example, had Napoleon won his wars, but it is hard to believe that it would have been more barbarous than it actually has been. Many of us, however, believed at the time and still believe a quarter of a century later that Nazism was an ultimate threat to everything decent in our lives, an ideology and a practice of political domination so murderous, so degrading even to those who might survive, that the consequences of its final victory in World War II were literally beyond calculation, immeasurably awful. We see it—and I don't use the phrase lightly—as evil objectified in the world, and in a form so potent and apparent that there could never have been anything to do but fight against it. It would be valuable to try to say precisely why we feel that way (avoiding the temptation simply to point) and to try also to make comparisons with other examples of evil in the world, with Stalinism above all. I cannot undertake either of these tasks. In this essay, I want only to ask how this perception of evil, which I am going to assume, affects our moral judgments in two cases: the decision, chiefly British, to go to war against Nazi Germany, and the decision, again chiefly British, to carry on that war by bombing German cities and terrorizing the civilian population.

II

To judge the decision to go to war, it is necessary to judge also the previous decisions not to go to war. The morality of appeasement is at issue, and this is a more complicated issue than it has sometimes appeared to be. Since some thirty million people died in the course of World War II, we should surely look with sympathy on all efforts to avoid the war altogether. But appeasement was an effort that failed, and thirty million people died. It is easy, then, to insist on what seems true enough, that the appeasers were an incredibly ignorant, complacent, and cowardly group of men, and to condemn their policy out of hand.[2] At the time, however, appeasement was supported by people

2. This is the line taken, for example, in two informative and highly plausible studies of appeasement: Martin Gilbert and Richard Gott, *The Appeasers* (London, 1963); and Margaret George, *The Warped Vision: British Foreign Policy 1933-1939* (Pittsburgh, 1965).

whom those adjectives don't describe, and for moral reasons. Not only for those reasons, of course, but they are my immediate concern. First among them was the accurate perception that the costs of the coming war would be carried to a very large degree by the civilian population. In part, this was a self-fulfilling prophecy: the British, not the Germans, planned and built a strategic bombing force capable of a sustained campaign against urban centers.[3] But it is not strange that a government building such a force, and others who knew about it, should be fearful of a war in which it might be used.

The second reason is equally important, if not as a motive, at least as a justification for appeasement. This was the sense, widespread in Britain (though not in France), that the Versailles Treaty had been unjust, that no permanent settlement could be founded on it, and that major changes were necessary in the map of Central Europe—for moral as well as political reasons. British foreign policy had already reflected this feeling in the 1920's (not only when the Tories were in power), and it continued to do so after 1933.[4] The national government, like the London *Times*, which consistently mirrored its policy, "saw no reason why an action that was justified by ethics and politics before January, 1933, should be held to be falsified by the events of the 30th of that month."[5] There is the crux of the matter, for the Nazi seizure of power did in fact change everything, politically and ethically, and if this was not immediately apparent, it ought to have become apparent long before 1939.

Yet Nazi demands were not so different from those frequently expressed by other Germans in the 1920's. Above all, they were similarly founded—this was the pretense—on the respectable and commonly accepted doctrine of national self-determination. There were, in fact, large German majorities in both the Sudetenland and Danzig, the cri-

3. "When war came, the Germans had no systematic plans for a strategic air offensive against Britain and . . . a bomber force of unimpressive quality" (Noble Frankland, *Bomber Offensive: The Devastation of Europe* [New York, 1970], p. 12).

4. See A.J.P. Taylor, *The Origins of the Second World War* (New York, 1968). Taylor's more controversial assertions about German foreign policy don't seem to me relevant to the moral questions I raise in this paper.

5. Quoted in A. L. Rowse, *All Souls and Appeasement* (London, 1961), p. 7, from the official history of the *Times*.

sis points of 1938 and 1939, and an adjustment of boundaries in these two areas must have seemed to many people a simple case of distributive justice: the land to its people or to the greater number of its people. It is only the further consequences of the distributive act that make it seem horrendous: all the people to the Nazi state.

There were, then, two ways of defending appeasement, by reference to the fear of war and to the right of self-determination. Both of these figure in the argument of a very intelligent little book published in 1939 by the Catholic writer Gerald Vann.[6] I am going to look closely at Vann's book, because it is the only attempt I have come across to apply just war theory directly to the problem of appeasement (and specifically to the Czech crisis of 1938). "The German government," Vann begins, "whether its claims were justified or not, or in what degree, had put itself in the wrong by its methods. There could be no doubt that an invasion, in the circumstances in which it was, in fact, threatened in September, would have been an unjust act of aggression." But he does not conclude from this that the act should have been resisted by the Czechs or the threat resolutely faced by the British. His book is a defense of Munich. He defends that short-lived settlement because of his fear of a general war, but also, I think, because German claims did seem to him at least partially justified: "It is wrong to commit aggression; it may be *equally wrong* to resist the demands that cause the aggression." The word "cause" is being used oddly here, but Vann's meaning could hardly have been lost on anyone reading his book in 1939, and it is stressed in his (unobjectionable) conclusion: "we should do everything . . . in our power to ensure that legitimate grievances are heard, legitimate demands satisfied, without loss of time. . . ."

It is the fear of war, however, rather than any view of justice, that leads Vann to propose what might be called the "Munich principle": "If a nation finds itself called upon to defend another nation which is unjustly attacked and to which it is bound by treaty, then it is bound to fulfill its obligations. . . . It may, however, be its right, and even its duty, to try to persuade the victim of aggression to avoid the ultimate evil of a general conflict by agreeing to terms less favorable than those

6. *Morality and War* (London, 1939). The quotations that follow are from pp. 31-32, 37, and 41; italics are mine.

which it can claim in justice . . . provided always that such a surrender of rights would not mean in fact a surrender once and for all to
the rule of violence." The "duty" here is simply "seek peace"—Hobbes's
first law of nature and presumably near the top of Catholic lists as
well (though Vann's phrase "ultimate evil" suggests that it is nearer
to the top than in fact it is). This is a duty that rulers of states certainly have; its performance is owed to their own people and to others
as well; and it may override other obligations established by international treaties and conventions. But the argument does require the
limiting clause at the end, which I would have thought applicable in
September 1938. That clause is worth examining, since its purpose is
obviously to tell us when to appease and when not—and so when to
make war and when not.

Let us imagine a state whose government strives to press its boundaries or its sphere of influence outward, a little bit here, a little bit
there, continually over a period of time, using force or the threat of
force as these appear necessary—a conventional "great power," in
other words. Certainly the people against whom the pressure is being
brought have a right to resist; allied states have a prima facie obligation to support their resistance. But appeasement, in either case, would
not, or not necessarily, be immoral; nor would it be difficult to construct a case where there would be a "duty" of the sort Vann suggests
to seek peace. (And the duty would seem, or be, greater if the pressure had some moral justification.) Appeasement would involve a
surrender to violence, but given a conventional power, it would not
or might not involve the absolute subjection of a particular group of
people to "the rule of violence." I take it that absolute subjection or
something like that is what Vann intends by "once and for all." He
cannot mean "forever," for governments fall, states decay, people rebel; we know nothing about forever. "Rule of violence" is a more difficult phrase. We can hardly set the moral limit of appeasement at the
point where it means yielding to greater physical force; it almost always means that. As a moral limit, the phrase must point to something
more unusual and more frightening: the rule of men committed to
the continual use of violence, to a policy of genocide, terrorism, or
enslavement. Then appeasement would be, quite simply, a failure to
resist evil in the world.

But I do not want to assert a general obligation to resist evil *any-where* in the world: one's work would never be done. I am still considering the "Munich principle" and its possible applications. The crucial question concerns the obligation of the people and rulers of a state like Britain to their weaker and threatened allies. The case of rulers probably has to be stressed, even when we are considering democracies, since rulers make decisions affecting others that are reviewed only after the fact and often inadequately by their own people and not at all by the people of allied states. How can they subject their fellow citizens to war because of "a quarrel in a faraway country between peoples of whom we know nothing"—even if the outcome or likely outcome of the quarrel is the triumph of evil (far away)?

The appropriate response to Chamberlain's extraordinary statement is to point out that the British knew a great deal about both Czechs and Germans. They knew (at any rate, the information was available to them) what sort of government the Germans had, what it was doing in its own country, and what it was likely to do in any country it came to rule.[7] And they knew that they had an alliance with the Czechs. Now it is possible to conceive of a world in which states have no relations whatsoever with one another, just as political theorists have sometimes constructed the mental image of a world of utterly dissociated individuals. Then there would be no obligations at all and no reason for any state or individual to be concerned about the moral condition of any other. It is not clear that one could even formulate the idea of a moral condition in such circumstances. But we do not live in either of these possible worlds. The British government had in fact obligations to the Czechs and good reason to worry about the moral condition of Germany. It might in good faith apply the "Munich principle" and seek to persuade the Czechs to yield to German demands only so long as yielding did not mean surrendering the Czechs "once and for all to the rule of violence." I find it very difficult to accept that any consideration for the safety of Britain or the peace of the world could override the obligation not to urge or to enforce such a surren-

7. British news correspondents in Germany sent home brutally honest reports. Geoffrey Dawson, editor of the *Times*, friend of Chamberlain, and one of the chief appeasers, "doctored the dispatches" in order to conceal the truth (George, *The Warped Vision*, p. 144).

der. The appeasement of Nazis at the expense of Czechs cannot be described as the overriding of obligations to the Czechs; it is their total renunciation. I can be committed to protect another man and yet urge that he surrender his purse to an armed thief; but I cannot urge that he surrender his life to a murderer, without denying my commitment altogether or breaking my faith.

It can't be said, however, that I am bound by my commitment to attack the murderer myself if I cannot do so effectively or if the likely outcome is my own destruction or the death of other people for whom I am responsible. Obligations to perform this or that specific action, to declare war or to fight, for example, can be overridden by conflicting duties.[8] But war is never the only alternative to appeasement: there are sanctions short of war (including the threat of war), and if nothing else is possible or other duties intervene, there remains at least the residual obligation not to make one's peace with the necessary surrender, to refuse to recognize or to admit that it is (in the usual sense of the term) "once and for all." Not to fight *now* may be justified or excusable, but "peace in our time" is obscene. We are bound to resist the evil that threatens or consumes our friends and allies at least to this extent: that we maintain our recognition of it as evil, declare our lasting hostility to it, prepare, by whatever means are appropriate, to fight against it.

Nor is it the case that whether we wage war against it or not depends simply on a calculation as to the number of lives likely to be lost if there is war or peace. Probably such calculations cannot be made with any degree of accuracy, but even if they were accurate, they would not be sufficient. Suppose that Nazism had triumphed unresisted in Europe and that its "rule of violence" had resulted in twenty million deaths before an internal coup had produced a "moderate" military regime and ended the reign of terror. But thirty million people (including some but not all of the first twenty million) died in the course of World War II. Foreknowledge of these outcomes would still not provide a sufficient reason for avoiding the war, because the human losses involved in a Nazi victory are not losses of life alone,

8. Thus, Britain declared war in September 1939, but made no move to help the Poles, her leaders arguing, probably rightly, that they had no means of doing so effectively and were compelled to buy time.

and the gains of war or peace cannot be measured simply in lives saved. I don't doubt that the rulers of the state have a very strong obligation to preserve the lives of their people, and so calculations of this sort should never be foreign to them. They have no right to a heroic disdain for such matters. But the social union is something more than a pact for the preservation of life; it is also a way of living together and (inevitably) of living with other peoples and other unions, and there is something here that needs to be preserved as well. In the choice between Nazi victory and resistance through war (when victory is possible), there is human degradation and enslavement on the one side and dignity, courage, and solidarity on the other. Here it is not possible simply to count. One relies on moral intuitions which can be defended and articulated, it seems to me, only in terms of a theory of evil.

But what is there to say if we are told that the Tory government of Britain, the cabinet of appeasement, did not regard the Nazi regime as evil? Many Tories seem in fact to have felt that the Nazis, while certainly very crude people, were doing what needed to be done in Central Europe, weeding out radicals, Jews, and trade unionists, building a bastion against the Bolsheviks.[9] Given such a view, appeasement is easily defensible, even if it means "persuading" Czechs (and others) to accept a settlement that is less than just or that is enforced by the Nazis with violence or the threat of violence. And then, those of us who regard the German regime as a force for evil (and especially those of us who are radicals, Jews, and trade unionists) must also regard the Tories as our enemies and fight them on the way to fighting the Nazis. We ought to distinguish, of course, between Tory complicity and Nazi crime.

There is a further question: What is there to say if the men who eventually do fight the Nazis do not regard them as evil—or do not regard the struggle against the evil of Nazism as their primary purpose? Theorists of the just war usually require that soldiers and their political and military commanders have just intentions, but this is one

9. "It was widely felt in British political and financial circles that such a useful bulwark against Communism as Hitler, deserved sympathy and support" (Paul Einzig, *Appeasement Before, During and After the War* [London, 1942], pp. 53-54).

of the most difficult and obscure features of their theory. Do they
mean, for example, *only* just intentions or just intentions among others? There are always others: men hope for many things from the end
of a war. "In 1939," writes a British historian, "Britain went to war,
not to destroy Nazism, but to prevent the further spread of German
domination in Europe."[10] At the time, the two purposes were served by
the same action and probably could not have been served in any other
way. The destruction of Nazism, one might say, was the foreseeable
side effect of the British war against German imperialism. Nor was it
an effect the British leaders were unwilling to have; many of them certainly hoped for it. But it was not their chief purpose. Now one could
oppose "German domination" even if there were no such thing as
Nazism, but I am not sure that one could justly oppose it by all-out
war. Does the existence of a Nazi regime in Germany justify the war?
I am inclined to think that it does, but I want more importantly to
insist that the war would not have been justified if its only purpose and
foreseeable effect had been to prevent Germany from winning a position in international affairs comparable to that of Britain herself in the
nineteenth century. Then the "Munich principle" might well apply,
and appeasement become a duty—if it were in fact the only way to
avoid the carnage of a worldwide conflict. And the same judgment
would have to be passed with reference to my next case, and with even
greater emphasis: the bombing of cities is surely not a justified response to a conventional imperialism.

III

The British have not, at least, tried to conceal the character of the
war they chose to fight. It was late in 1940 that the decision to bomb
cities was made. A directive issued in June of that year had "specifically laid down that targets had to be identified and aimed at. Indiscriminate bombing was forbidden." In November, after the German
raid on Coventry, "Bomber Command was instructed simply to aim at
the center of a city." What had once been called indiscriminate bomb-

---

10. Martin Gilbert, *Britain and Germany Between the Wars* (London, 1964),
p. 70. Gilbert may mean only that the British would not have gone to war, and
did not, to destroy Nazism *in Germany*—a point which raises many difficult questions that I cannot consider here.

ing was now required, and by early 1942 aiming at military or industrial targets within cities was barred: "the aiming points are to be the built-up areas, *not*, for instance, the dockyards or aircraft factories."[11] The purpose of the raids was explicitly declared to be the destruction of civilian morale. Following the famous minute of Lord Cherwell in 1942, the means to this demoralization was further specified: working-class residential areas were the prime targets. Cherwell thought it possible to render a third of the German population homeless by the middle of 1943.[12]

Now the rule against the deliberate killing of civilians (noncombatants) in wartime is very old and its moral value widely recognized. Its application to the problems of aerial bombardment was, in 1940, fairly recent, not yet incorporated in international treaties and conventions, but there could be no doubt as to the practical requirements of the rule, broadly understood. Thus an international commission of jurists meeting in The Hague in the 1920's concluded that: "Aerial bombardment destined to terrorize the civilian population, or to destroy or damage private property which has no military character, or to wound noncombatants, is prohibited."[13] These prohibitions and the rule from which they follow can be defended in a variety of ways, of which I will single out two, without attempting to choose between them. It can be defended first as a limit upon the destructive force of warfare which is generally useful to mankind—useful over time, that is, since its violation might at any given moment serve the interests of one party or another. Doubtless, the precise marking of the limit, the definition of noncombatant, proves in every war a troublesome and ultimately an arbitrary matter. But this is not a satisfactory criticism of the argument for the utility of the rule. There are conventional guidelines that can be followed and, what is more important, clear cases on either side of any particular disputed line. It is the acceptance

---

11. Frankland, *Bomber Offensive*, pp. 24ff. I should note that the Americans, when they came into the war, tended to favor precision bombing—though not for moral reasons. American pilots did join in attacks on cities (Dresden, for example) and later made terror bombing their policy in the war against Japan. But I will confine myself here to a discussion of the British decision.

12. The story of the Cherwell minute is told, most unsympathetically, in C. P. Snow, *Science and Government* (Cambridge, Mass., 1961).

13. Quoted in Vann, *Morality and War*, p. 50.

of these conventions and the recognition of the clear cases that is generally useful, and that is all the rule requires.

The rule can also be defended because of the intrinsic value it attaches to human personality. It requires that we pay attention to what men and women are actually doing, that we regard and treat them as responsible agents. So we fight soldiers, who are armed and trained and committed to fight us (whether or not they are actually engaged in combat). But we do not fight civilians who, whatever their hopes for our destruction, are not engaged in bringing it about. Obviously, this defense is challenged by the claim, frequently made, that there are no noncombatants in modern war. That claim is certainly exaggerated (small children are always, one might say eternally, noncombatants), but I am inclined to think it is false unless stated very modestly indeed. In modern war, there are fewer noncombatants than ever before. This minimal claim follows from the conventional recognition that munitions workers are at least partial combatants, subject to attack in their factories (though not at home)—for modern war requires a very large industrial plant. But there remain vast numbers of people who are not engaged in any activity properly called warmaking. In the words of the philosopher G.E.M. Anscombe, they "are not fighting and not engaged in supplying those who are with the means of fighting."[14] Intentional attacks on them do not seem to me properly called combat. Such attacks victimize and exploit innocent people, turning them into means to an end which, it must be stressed again, they were not opposing in any miltary way, though they may have opposed it in other ways when they were alive. In the bombing of cities, civilians are effectively claimed as hostages by the enemy and, like more conventional hostages, are degraded from moral agents to human pawns even before they are murdered.

It should be clear that I have been using words like "responsible," "innocent," and "moral agent" in a special sense in the preceding paragraph. These are all words that can be used in a perfectly ordinary way with reference to criminal action. But war, even when it is an aggressive war, is not necessarily the criminal action of soldiers or munitions workers. With reference to the war itself, they may not be

14. G.E.M. Anscombe, *Mr. Truman's Degree* (privately printed, n.d.). This is one of the best defenses of the immunity of noncombatants.

agents at all and not personally responsible. And then they are innocent in the ordinary sense of that word, which means that they cannot
rightly be punished. But they can be resisted and attacked because, as
Miss Anscombe says, they are *engaged in harming* (even if the harming is justified). Their own options may be radically limited: they can
only hide, flee, surrender, or work and fight. Nevertheless, we treat
them (and, what is more important, the others, who are not engaged
in harming) as persons in the only way we can, given the conditions
of war—by paying attention to the activites in which they are actually
engaged. In peacetime, we "pay attention" differently, looking to past
actions, intentions, extenuations, and so on. I don't want to argue,
however, that these last considerations do not figure at all in our wartime thinking. I shall suggest later on one way in which they cut across
the combatant-noncombatant distinction.

A number of reasons have been given for the British decision to
attack German cities. From the beginning, the attacks were defended
as reprisals for the German blitz. This defense was thought to be
politically popular and was energetically argued by the Prime Minister, who apparently also believed that reprisal raids were necessary
for British morale. "The British airforce," he promised in a radio
broadcast in 1941, would make "the German people taste and gulp
each month a sharper dose of the miseries they have showered upon
mankind."[15] It is interesting to note that a Gallup poll of this same
year showed that "the most determined demand for [reprisal raids]
came from Cumberland, Westmorland, and the North Riding of York-
shire, rural areas barely touched by bombing, where some 3/4 of the
population wanted them. In central London, conversely, the proportion was only forty-five percent."[16] Doubtless, Churchill had more political support in Cumberland, Westmorland, and the North Riding
than in central London, but there was room for leadership here and
obvious counterarguments to be made to the reprisal defense. I won't
attempt to make them now, since I want to concentrate on the military
justifications for terror bombing, which, we must assume, were para-
mount in Churchill's mind also. I should note, however, that the de-

15. Quoted in Angus Calder, *The People's War: Britain—1939-1945* (New
York, 1969), p. 491.
16. *Ibid.*, p. 229.

fense in terms of civilian morale, which is or might be a military
justification, seems highly implausible. The news that Germany was
being bombed was certainly glad tidings in Britain, but as late as 1944
the overwhelming majority of Britishers still believed that the raids
were directed solely against military targets.[17] Presumably that is what
they wanted to believe—there was quite a bit of evidence to the contrary—but that says something about the character of their morale.
(It should also be said that the campaign against terror bombing, run
largely by pacifists, won very little popular support.)

I can only discuss the military arguments in a general way. There
was a great deal of dispute at the time, largely about technical matters: the calculations of the Cherwell minute, for example, were
sharply attacked by a group of men whose opposition to terror bombing may well have had moral grounds, but whose position was never,
to the best of my knowledge, stated in moral terms. These disputes are
not my concern here, except insofar as the doubts they raised enter
(as they must) into political and moral calculations. First of all, then,
it became clear early in the war that, given the navigational devices
then available, no target smaller than a fairly large city could reasonably be aimed at. A study made in 1941 indicated that of those planes
that actually did attack their target (that is, two-thirds of the attacking force), only one-third dropped their bombs within five miles of
the point aimed at.[18] Once this was known, it would seem dishonest
to claim that the intended target was, say, *this* aircraft factory and
that the indiscriminate destruction around it was only an unintended,
if foreseeable, consequence of the justified attempt to stop the produc-
tion of planes. What was really unintended but foreseeable was that
the factory itself would probably escape harm. If strategic bombing
was to make any sense, one would have to plan the destruction one
could (and did) cause. Lord Cherwell's minute was an effort at such
planning. In fact, of course, navigational devices were rapidly im-
proved as the war went on, and the bombing of specific military targets continued, receiving at times (before the June 1944 invasion of
France, for example) top priority and severely limiting Bomber Command's ability to destroy cities. Today many experts believe that the

17. *Ibid.*, p. 491.
18. Frankland, *Bomber Offensive*, pp. 38-39.

war might have been ended sooner had there been a greater concentration of air power against targets like the German oil refineries.[19] But the decision to bomb cities was made at a time when victory was, literally, not in sight and the specter of defeat ever present. And it was made when no other decision seemed possible if there was to be any serious offensive against Germany.

Bomber Command was the only offensive weapon available to the British in those frightening years, and I expect there is some truth to the notion that it was used simply because it was available. "It was the only force in the west," writes Sir Arthur Harris, chief of Bomber Command from 1942 until the end of the war, "which could take offensive action . . . against Germany, our only means of getting at the enemy in a way that would hurt at all."[20] Offensive action could have been postponed until (or in the hope of) some more favorable time; there was even considerable military pressure for postponement. Harris was hardpressed to keep his Command together in the face of repeated calls for tactical air support (which would have been coordinated with ground action largely defensive in character, since the German armies were still advancing everywhere). Sometimes, in his memoirs, he allows himself to sound like a bureaucrat defending his function and his office, but obviously he was also defending a certain conception of how the war might best be fought. He did not believe that the weapons he commanded should be used because he commanded them. He believed that the tactical use of bombers could not win the war and that the destruction of cities ("the only possible policy for Bomber Command at that time") could win it.[21] That is an argument requiring careful examination. It was apparently accepted by the Prime Minister. "The bombers alone," Churchill had said as early as September 1940, "provide the means of victory."[22]

The bombers alone—that poses the issue very starkly and perhaps wrongly, given the disputes over strategy to which I have already re-

19. *Ibid.*, p. 134.

20. Sir Arthur Harris, *Bomber Offensive* (London, 1947), p. 74. Harris claims to have been skeptical about the prospect of civilian demoralization; he favored the bombing of cities because he thought that was the only way to destroy German industry.

21. *Ibid.*, p. 88.

22. Calder, *The People's War*, p. 229.

ferred. At the very least, Churchill's statement suggested a certainty
to which neither he nor anyone else had any right. But the issue can
be stated so as to accommodate a certain skepticism and to permit
even the most sophisticated among us to indulge in a common fan-
tasy: suppose I sat in the seat of power and had to decide whether
or not to use Bomber Command. Suppose further that unless bombers
were used, and used (in the only way they could be used systematically and effectively) against cities, the probability that Germany
would eventually be defeated would be radically reduced. It makes no
sense to fill in figures; I have no notion what the probabilities actually
were or even how they should have been calculated had our present
knowledge been available, nor any precise understanding of how different figures would affect the moral argument. But it does seem to
me that the more certain a German victory appeared to be in the
absence of a bomber offensive, the more justifiable was the decision
to launch the offensive.

Before developing this argument, however, I want to deal with a
more frequently encountered version of the military defense, heavily
stressed by Harris. Here the emphasis is not on the probability of victory itself, but rather on the time and price of victory. Bomber Command, it is claimed, ended the war sooner than it would otherwise
have been ended and, despite the immense civilian casualties it inflicted, at a lower cost in human lives. Assuming this claim to be true
(I have already indicated that precisely opposite claims are made by
some historians and strategists), it is nevertheless not sufficient to
justify the bombing.[23] The utility of the general rule cannot be denied
on the basis of evidence that the rule is harmful in this or that present
case, since it has presumably been beneficial in the past and its ero-
sion or rejection might be disastrous for the future. At the very least,
evidence would have to be presented that looked to the future and
suggested that the long-term balance was in favor of life and not
death. Arguments more or less of this sort were made at the time (not
by Harris); they commonly took the form of a kind of deterrence theory. Bombing, suggested George Orwell, for example, brought the true

23. See John C. Ford, S. J., "The Morality of Obliteration Bombing," for a
well-argued response to this claim. Ford's essay, first published in 1944, is reprinted in *War and Morality*, ed. Richard A. Wasserstrom (Belmont, Cal., 1970).

character of modern warfare home to the civilian population, to all those people who supported the war, even enjoyed it, only because they did not feel its effects; now they felt them, and so war was less likely in the future.[24] I doubt that there is enough evidence for this argument actually to lead anybody to begin bombing cities; it is an apology after the fact, and not a very convincing one.

In any case, the defense of the rule, even the ultilitarian defense, need not be concerned only with the preservation of life. The presumed benefits of the rule reach further than that; there is much else that we might plausibly want to preserve—the quality of our lives, for example, our civilization and morality, our collective abhorrence of murder, even when it seems to serve, as it always does, some narrow purpose. Then the deliberate slaughter of innocent men and women cannot be justified simply because it saves the lives of other men and women. I suppose it is possible to imagine cases that make that last assertion hard: where the number of people involved is small; the probability of saving six, say, at the cost of killing one, is very high; the events are hidden from the public eye; and so on. I won't discuss such cases here, but only suggest that they are somehow put out of our minds by the sheer scale of the calculations necessary in World War II. To kill 278,966 civilians (the number is made up) in order to avoid the deaths of an unknown but probably larger number of civilians and soldiers is surely a bizarre, godlike, frightening, and horrendous act. This is not simply because no one can possibly know enough to justify murder on such a scale (he would have to know everything), but also because the knowledge he claims to have and the evil he hopes to avoid are neither of them radical or extreme enough even to explain his action. He is guilty of a drastic attack on our entire civilization, and his only defense is that he hoped to save and may have saved some of our lives.[25]

But suppose that civilization itself is really at stake, that the question is not the price of victory, but victory simply, and *our* defeat will

24. See his *Tribune* columns for 1944, in *The Collected Essays, Journalism, and Letters of George Orwell*, ed. Sonia Orwell and Ian Angus (New York, 1968), Vol. 3.

25. Nor is it wrong to suggest, for reasons given above, that the lives involved have to be weighed differently: killing civilians is worse than killing soldiers.

be a triumph not for some conventional *them*, but specifically for the Nazis. With this knowledge in mind, I find myself moving uneasily toward the decision Churchill made, though not, perhaps, for his (or all of his) reasons. Given the view of Nazism I have been assuming, the issue takes this form: Should I wager this determinate crime against that immeasurable evil? Obviously, if there is some other way of avoiding the evil or even a reasonable chance of another way, I must wager differently or elsewhere. But I can never hope to be sure; even if I wager and win, it is still possible that I was wrong, that my crime was unnecessary to victory. But I can argue that I studied the case as closely as I was able, took the best advice I could find, and so on. If this is right, and my perception of evil not hysterical or self-serving, then surely I must wager. There is no option; the risk otherwise is too great. My own action is determinate, of course, only as to its immediate consequences, while the rule which bars such acts looks to the future, but I dare to say that there will be no future or no foreseeable future for civilization and its rules unless I accept the burdens of criminality.[26]

But if my crime is not determinate at all, if we imagine Sir Arthur Harris, for example, in possession of and ready to use the first atomic bomb, then the risks are probably no longer acceptable. And it is no longer necessary or morally possible to accept the risks as soon as the threat of immeasurable evil passes. That is why it is so easy to condemn the attack on Dresden in 1945, which killed so many thousands of people and may or may not have hastened the end of the war by a few days: there was no longer even a remote chance of a Nazi victory.[27] Indeed, the worst of the destruction of German cities took place after the greatest danger was long past and cannot be defended with the sorts of arguments I have been using.

All this has been very hard to write, and one of the most difficult and puzzling features of the argument has until now remained hidden. Is there any reason to find the moral burdens of the bombing more acceptable because the cities bombed were German? Allied

26. I explore what it means to "accept the burdens of criminality" in the preceding essay, "The Problem of Dirty Hands," pp. 62ff.

27. The story of the Dresden raid is told in David Irving, *The Destruction of Dresden* (New York, 1965).

planes did bomb French cities and kill many Frenchmen, but they always did this while bombing what were or were thought to be military targets.[28] They did not aim at the "built-up areas" of French cities. Suppose they had: the theory that distinguishes combatants from noncombatants does not distinguish Allied from enemy noncombatants, not at least with regard to the question of their murder. Yet I would find the wager far more difficult to undertake or defend if, through some strange combination of circumstances, it required the deliberate slaughter of French civilians. It is at this point that considerations of responsibility and moral agency (in the ordinary sense) necessarily enter our thinking. They do not justify bombing cities or killing civilians, but they may explain or help explain why, assuming some other reason for doing these things, one only aims at certain cities and intends to kill certain civilians. The argument here is perhaps analogous to that general view of punishment which holds that one does not punish people because they are guilty, but that one nevertheless only punishes guilty people. I do not mean to suggest some sort of collective guilt shared by German combatants and noncombatants alike. But it does make sense to say that there were a great many more people in German cities responsible, in however diminished a degree, for the evil of Nazism than there were in French cities. And that may be sufficient to explain the feeling I have alluded to above, which other people probably share and are as uneasy about as I am.[29]

IV

It is undoubtedly reckless to talk of immeasurable evil. Someone will surely come along and suggest a way of measuring the Nazi

28. For a description of an American air attack on a French town, see Howard Zinn (a participant in the attack), *The Politics of History* (Boston, 1970), pp. 250-275.

29. The issue might be clarified if we imagine a German city in which no children lived and where all the adults had actively supported the Nazi Party. Whatever punishment ought to be imposed on those adults surely ought not to be imposed on them by bombing their city. Bombing the city would be a crime, if only because it would be punishing the inhabitants without a trial. Yet if it appeared that Nazism could be defeated in no other way, one would hesitate less before committing that crime than if there were innocent people among the inhabitants of the city. (This example was suggested to me at a discussion of my paper by members of the Society for Ethical and Legal Philosophy.)

threat to civilized values. What is even more likely is that many people will insist that there have been numerous threats no less serious, whether measurable or not, in recent political history. I am prepared to argue that last point. But it is probably more important to recognize that disagreements will in fact occur, and other men at other times will be tempted to make the ultimate wager. *Who would refuse to fight at Armageddon?* Unfortunately, there are always going to be soldiers on the battlefields of Blenheim who think they are standing at Armageddon and who are prepared to risk some awful crime for the sake of victory. That is why moral rules are so important and why they are usually stated and probably should be stated (in international law, for example) in absolute terms.

It is tempting, though it would be wrong, to say that Nazism requires us to recognize the limits of the absolute. It is more prosaic, and probably right, to say, as my previous arguments require, that the rules are not absolute. They establish very strong presumptions against certain sorts of actions, like the deliberate killing of noncombatants. These are not irrebuttable presumptions, however, even if the conventional rebuttals have to be rejected. It is possible to imagine situations where one would break the rules and accept the moral consequences of doing so. And it is possible to find such situations in recent history. I realize that I have not suggested criteria by which they might be recognized; that still needs to be done, and while it will obviously not be difficult to offer a formal description of immeasurability, the substance of evil is much harder to grasp and explain, at least for secular minds like my own. All I have done here is to single out World War II as a case where a wager against the rules might be morally required. That is what makes World War II different.

SANFORD LEVINSON

Responsibility for Crimes of War

Because it is apparently intolerable for men to admit the key role of accident, of ignorance, and of unplanned processes in their affairs, the leader serves a vital function by personifying and reifying the processes. As an individual, he can be praised and blamed and given "responsibility" in a way that processes cannot. Incumbents of high public office therefore become objects of acclaim for the satisfied, scapegoats for the unsatisfied, and symbols of aspirations or of whatever is opposed. To them are constantly ascribed careful weighing of alternatives and soul-searching decisions. That the premises for the decisions are largely supplied and screened by others and the decision itself frequently predetermined by a succession of subordinates' decisions is not publicized. Decision-making at the highest levels is not so much literal policy-making as dramaturgy.[1]

. . . a deeper analytical understanding of [the etiology of American policy in Vietnam] is not likely to be reached by a searcher committed and determined to see the conflict and our part in it as "a tragedy without villains," war crimes without criminals, lies without liars, a process of immaculate deception.[2]

Murray Edelman points to a central difficulty present in any analysis of decision-making within large, complex organizations: whether

Acknowledgment is made to Prof. John Barton and to Prof. Michael Walzer, whose seminars at Stanford aided considerably the formulation of the ideas presented here.

1. Murray Edelman, *The Symbolic Uses of Politics* (Urbana, 1964), p. 78.
2. Daniel Ellsberg, *Papers on the War* (New York, 1972), p. 129.

the organization be the American government, General Motors, or Stanford University, a search for discrete individuals who can be allocated "responsibility" for the institution's activities in other than a formal sense often proves frustrating.[3] Almost inevitably the serious student will subordinate the search for such discrete individuals to a study of the institutional structures which seem to generate policies and behavior quite independent of conscious decisions.

Nor is the lawyer in a much better position. There seems to be an inverse relationship between the number of individuals involved in a transaction or event and the efficacy of traditional legal analysis as a mode of comprehending it. Once beyond a strictly two-person interaction—be it a murder, contract, or automobile accident, we enter the world of respondeat superior, agency, aiding and abetting, or conspiracy law. Even that law loses its power as anything more than a formal analysis when the individuals involved pass beyond a small number. And of no area is this more true than criminal law. We may accept wide-ranging imputations of responsibility for tort liability because of our belief that, when all is said and done, the individual or corporation deemed "responsible," even if not properly viewed as a causal agent, is not really paying a heavy cost because of an ability to spread the general costs among customers, etc. More to the point even than this economic analysis is the fact that civil liability usually does not carry with it any finding of moral inadequacy. "What distinguishes a criminal from a civil sanction," as Henry Hart argued, "and all that distinguishes it . . . is the judgment of community condemnation which accompanies and justifies its imposition."[4] Thus, paradoxically, a theory which justifies an automobile owner's being made responsible for a $100,000 tort liability actually caused by the driver using his car proves inadequate to uphold that same owner's being fined $500 for the drunken driving behind the accident. And this is so, even if the

3. The most important recent analysis of problems facing the decision analyst is Graham T. Allison's *Essence of Decision: Explaining the Cuban Missile Crisis* (Boston, 1971). A critique of Allison that focuses on the issue of responsibility is Stephen D. Krasner, "Are Bureaucracies Important? (Or Allison Wonderland)," *Foreign Policy* 7, (Summer 1972): 159-179.

4. Henry M. Hart, "The Aims of the Criminal Law," *Law and Contemporary Problems* 23, no. 3 (Summer 1958): 404.

former, in a given case, would destroy economically the individual or business made liable.

Great difficulties emerge when one considers the question of criminal responsibility for actions occurring within an organizational context. If we wish to engage in communal condemnation of such acts, against whom should the opprobrium be directed? It is no answer, of course, to say only the organization itself, for this simply begs the question, as I shall show below, of whether or not it is just to punish everyone connected with it. No sanction can be directed at an organization—whether the method chosen is a fine or dissolution—without also affecting at least some of the individuals with ties to the entity.[5]

Most domestic criminal law avoids these problems by focusing only on acts occurring within nonorganizational settings (unless a conspiracy be regarded as an organization). International public law, on the other hand, focuses especially on the acts of organizations, particularly those known as states. This difference is a product of experience rather than of logical necessity. There are domestic criminal laws which do apply to collectivities, and the war trials which are the subject of this essay are the most dramatic attempts to invoke the sanctions of international law against given individuals. We are, nevertheless, most comfortable analyzing conduct which occurs outside of formal institutional settings. Moreover, in evaluating individuals we tend to judge most confidently their adherence to well established norms of interpersonal relations, such as individual honesty. Thus a public official who accepts bribes is condemned because of the personal flaws his conduct is presumed to reveal. If, on the other hand, he participates in carrying out criminal policies of his government, there is much greater hesitancy to condemn him. The latter is viewed as a "political judgment," about which the widest norms of toleration are encouraged, and not as a genuinely "personal act" indicating his moral character.

5. One of the clearest examples of this point is the punishment by the National Collegiate Athletic Association of the University of California at Berkeley for violations in its athletic programs. Although the coaches responsible for the misdeeds are no longer connected with the University, no team representing the University can participate in a post-season event. The greatest victims of this sanction are eighteen- and nineteen-year-old athletes who were in high school when the violations occurred.

The problem of "war crimes," of course, raises these problems in an
especially vivid way. Following World War II there was obvious interest in punishing those who were responsible for the acts of the Nazi
state,[6] and the subsequent trials of alleged war criminals raised very
sharply the problems involved in trying to assess the responsibility of
a given individual relative to a very complex scheme of organizational
behavior.[7] What follows are a description and analysis of the notions
of responsibility that were put forth at four of the war crimes trials
and an examination of their implications regarding the actions of
American officials concerning the Vietnam War. The advisability of
the post-World War II trials or the merits of the particular counts
brought forth at Nuernberg[8] will not, however, be discussed.

I

Before beginning the central analysis, it is desirable to explain why
the question of individual responsibility cannot be escaped by simple
reference to corporate guilt. It has been pointed out that, prior to
Nuernberg, the standard sanctions for violation of the laws of warfare
had been either military reprisals or, more significantly for our purposes, reparations imposed by the victorious states upon the losers.[9]
Now such reparations might be defensible if they were viewed merely
as tort damages; i.e., compensation paid a victim for injuries received

6. Trials were also held, of course, in regard to Japanese leaders. Except for
reference to the *Yamashita* case, 327 U.S. 1 (1946), below, I am ignoring those
trials. The principal reason is that they have been subjected to more persuasive
criticism as to their fairness than I think is the case with the Nuernberg trials.
See Richard Minear, *Victor's Justice: The Tokyo War Crimes Trial* (Princeton,
1971). In any case there is certainly nothing in those trials which would make
responsibility more *limited* than the analysis presented here.

7. I will not be concerned in this paper with the quite separate problems of
the defenses of obedience to superior orders or of the "act of state" doctrine. See
Yoram Dinstein, *The Defense of "Obedience to Superior Orders," in International
Law* (Leyden, 1965).

8. I have adopted throughout this paper the spelling "Nuernberg" because it
is used by the Government Printing Office in its edition of the *Trials of War
Criminals Before the Nuernberg Military Tribunals Under Control Council Law
No. 10,* hereafter cited, with volume and date, as *T.W.C.*

9. William V. O'Brien, "The Nuremberg Principles," from James Finn, ed.,
A Conflict of Loyalties, reprinted in Richard A. Falk, ed., *The Vietnam War and
International Law* 3: *The Widening Context* (Princeton, 1972), p. 201.

because of an event having some connection with the defendant. Yet there is no moral opprobrium attached to the defendant in such a situation; he, or indeed someone else with some requisite relationship to the compensation-giver, simply did not exercise "due care" in the given situation.

Such an analysis, however, hardly does justice to the notion of war *crimes*. Whatever else is the case, if one takes the notion of war crimes seriously, then the conduct in question is outrageous and richly deserving of condemnation. Moreover, those who commit war crimes are viewed as morally flawed.[10]

---

10. I should admit at this point that this essay begs a major question, i.e., whether it *is* necessarily immoral to commit war crimes. There are at least two ways of approaching this question. The traditional way is to reject the notion that any specific mode of conduct is *absolutely* forbidden, but instead to argue that "military necessity" would justify the breaking of any given rule in a given situation. See Marshall Cohen's critique of Telford Taylor's *Nuremberg and Vietnam: An American Tragedy* (Chicago, 1970), in *The Yale Law Journal* 80, no. 7 (June, 1971): 1492-1500, as well as the essays by Nagel, Brandt, and Hare in Part I of this volume. Thus it becomes impossible to commit a "war crime" if in fact it was "necessary" to commit an act otherwise labeled as such. This is obviously an unsatisfactory resolution of the problem for it seems to admit that an official is entitled to do whatever is necessary to win a battle or war. Even if this be tempered by the recognition that such latitude is allowed only if the cause for which the war is being fought is in fact just, then this simply pushes the argument back one step, so that the motives impelling the conflict must be evaluated. And, note well, we then analyze not the given conduct, such as torturing prisoners, but rather the wider justification of the war itself. See, for example, the preceding essay in this volume, pp. 85ff., by Michael Walzer, "World War II: Why Was This War Different?" But in that situation, what makes the official a war criminal is the injustice of the war itself, even if we may be additionally appalled by the particular means with which that war is carried out.

A second way of approaching the question is to strike more basically at the notion that *criminal* conduct is necessarily *immoral*. That is, the notion of criminality may be positivistically derived from the prohibition of given conduct by a formal legal system. But it is a separate question whether or not such conduct is immoral. Thus many philosophers can easily admit that Martin Luther King or the Berrigan brothers are criminals, but go on to deny that they are also immoral because they broke the law. Yet if we can justify civil disobedience in the one case, must we not at least admit the possibility that a "war criminal" could present an analogous case? Is it necessarily a contradiction in terms that,

Collective criminal punishment is in principle open to the charge that it violates fundamental standards of fairness by being "overinclusive": the category of individuals actually stigmatized or otherwise treated as criminal would include some who could successfully defend

---

in a given context, we might wish to *honor* a war criminal if we viewed the cause for which he broke the law as just? This question obviously overlaps with that in the paragraph above.

There is a still more subversive way of making this point, and that is to attack the moral coherence of the present laws of warfare. The most provocative statement of this position is Richard Wasserstrom, "The Laws of War," *Monist* 56, no. 1 (January, 1972): 1-19. See also his "The Relevance of Nuremberg," which follows in this volume, pp. 134ff. He argues basically that the present laws of war are morally senseless. For example, it is a war crime to bomb a military hospital, but not to bomb sleeping soldiers well back of the front lines. Why? It is a war crime to remove works of art from an occupied country to the museums of the victor, but not to saturate enemy citizens with bombs. Can this distinction be defended?

Wasserstrom's point must be read in the context of Hart's argument quoted above. Hart *assumes* the existence of a single community organized around a coherent moral code reflected in its criminal law. His notion of condemnation makes no sense otherwise. But the code under which crimes of war are defined may be incoherent. Thus I take it that Wasserstrom would not deny that bombers of military hospitals *should* be condemned; he would simply add that so should bombers of cities. A criminal law which punishes one and not the other, to adopt his own metaphor, is comparable to one which sanctions petty theft but is silent as to grand theft. Half a loaf may be worse than none if there is no principle by which one can defend selecting out only those activities punished by the present laws of war. It would be better to focus clearly on the *morality* of warfare and to speak unequivocally of moral condemnation than to pretend that the category of "war crimes" or "war criminals" is meaningful. The President who ordered the bombing of Hanoi over Christmas 1972 is surely more condemnable, even if perhaps not a "criminal," than some soldier in the field who in frustration murders a prisoner of war. To focus on the latter as a "criminal" while viewing the former as "merely" immoral is to reverse the priorities of sensible discussion. For an example of such a reversal, see Joseph W. Bishop, Jr., "The Question of War Crimes," *Commentary* 54, no. 6 (December 1972): 85-92. (Perhaps it is worth adding that I think that Nixon's conduct in ordering the bombing *is* criminal because no plausible claim of "military necessity" can be offered for it, but the main point is that its immorality would not in the least be lessened by a judgment that it was not criminal.)

This paper accepts for the moment Hart's assumptions, but I would be less than honest if I denied that the questions outlined above trouble me deeply. A complete theory of war criminality would certainly have to answer them rather than relegate them to a footnote.

themselves, if given the chance to do so.[11] This objection to collective responsibility is, obviously, independent of the fact that it may be more practical or efficient to label everyone connected with a group "responsible." Those who would say that the answer to the problem of war crimes is simply to extract fines from the state at fault would not, I suspect, also defend the proposition that, because "practical," it would therefore have been just to fine everyone arrested in the 1971 May Day demonstration in Washington $25, even though the arrests were based in part on a conscious policy of "overinclusiveness" decided upon by police and Department of Justice officials, because, after all, many of those arrested *were* guilty, and the others could afford to pay $25. The analogy is more apt than it might appear because reparations are collected through general tax revenues, and it would always be legitimate for a given individual to ask why it is just to fine *him* for something he did not do, i.e., commit a war crime.

Confirmation of sorts is provided for this distaste regarding collective punishment by the very judgment of the International Military Tribunal concerning its finding that certain German organizations were criminal in themselves. The imputation of collective criminality was immediately followed by qualifications drawn from the traditional criminal law: "Since the declaration with respect to the organizations and groups, will . . . fix the criminality of its members, that definition should exclude persons who had no knowledge of the criminal purposes or acts of the organization and those who were drafted by the State for membership, unless they were personally implicated in the commission of acts declared criminal. . . . Membership alone is not enough to come within the scope of these declarations."[12] One can compare this language with decisions of the United States Supreme Court limiting liability under the Smith Act to "knowing membership" and participation in the Communist Party.[13]

11. See Joseph Tussman and Jacobus tenBroek, "The Equal Protection of the Laws," *California Law Review* 37, no. 3 (September 1949): 341-381, especially pp. 351-352 on "overinclusiveness."

12. *Trials of the Major War Criminals before the International Military Tribunal* 22 (1948), p. 500. Hereafter cited as *I.M.T.*

13. Yates v. United States, 354 U.S. 298 (1957); Scales v. United States, 367 U.S. 203 (1961).

To say that every German or every American is "guilty" for every act committed by persons acting under the authority of their respective States rests on a host of begged questions.[14] And even if one accepts, for the sake of argument, the notion of collective guilt, we can still distinguish among degrees of responsibility. It would be unjust for everyone to have to pay the *same* fine for war crimes unless we assume equal guilt or assume that guilt varied directly by income, so that the progressive income tax would be an adequate collection device. The only viable defense of collective reparations then is to adopt the torts analogy, though at the price of removing the sting of moral outrage that underlies criminal adjudication. Indeed even the torts analogy rests on a begged question—the relationship between "fault" and liability. If we emphasize the necessity for a linkage, then even the torts analogy could scarcely support collective reparation without proof of fault.[15]

We are thus impaled on the horns of a dilemma: to adopt collective responsibility is either to commit an injustice or to undermine the community condemnation on which the criminal law rests and which especially should be the basis for the punishment of war crimes. If one wants to preserve the force of the notion of war *criminality*, he must find discrete criminals or else argue that in fact everyone *is* guilty and deserving of punishment.

14. The most recent philosophical analysis is Joel Feinberg, "Collective Responsibility," in *Doing and Deserving* (Princeton, 1970), pp. 222-251. A classic polemical attack on the notion is Dwight MacDonald, "The Responsibility of Peoples," in *Memoirs of a Revolutionist* (Cleveland, 1957), pp. 33-106.

15. For a survey of the problem of criminal liability of business corporations, see "Comment: Increasing Community Control over Corporate Crime—A Problem in the Law of Sanctions," *Yale Law Journal* 71, no. 2 (December, 1961): 280-306.

As to the complexities even of collective tort liability, I offer the following, reprinted in its entirety from *The Wall Street Journal*, 17 January 1973, p. 1: "MORE BUCKS FOR THE BANG: Someone left an explosive on the baseball field in Estherville, Iowa, after a public fireworks display in 1969. William Rosenau, then 14 years old, happened by and lit it. It exploded, blowing off three of William's fingers. A court found the town of 8,108 negligent and awarded William a judgment of $94,676. To raise the money, Estherville is increasing property taxes."

II

I shall be considering the judgments of four trials held at Nuernberg following World War II. Those four are the Trial of the Major War Criminals, held before the International Military Tribunal (IMT), which consisted of judges appointed by the four major Allied powers, in addition to three trials held under the aegis of Allied Control Council Law No. 10, by which the individual powers were given authority to prosecute "lesser" alleged war criminals. These three trials, held before American tribunals, are usually called "The Ministries Case,"[16] "The High Command Case,"[17] and "The Hostage Case."[18] All four of the cases featured multiple defendants; all four included defendants who were acquitted as well as more numerous ones who were found guilty. In this section the focus will be on general doctrine which can be derived from the judgments. In the following section the judgment of a specific individual, Ernst von Weizsaecker, will be examined so that the application of the doctrines can be better understood.

The trial before the IMT is, of course, the most famous of the war trials, largely because of the inherent drama provided by the celebrity of the defendants. Here were Goering, Rosenberg, von Ribbentrop, Speer, and eighteen others, most of whom were "household words" to the communities involved in fighting the war. Precisely because of the rank of the defendants, however, the judgment is relatively unilluminating from the point of view of this paper, for there was, in fact, little difficulty in proving the criminal behavior of most of them, save only for the three who were acquitted—Schacht, von Papen, and Fritzsche.[19]

16. *T.W.C.* 14 (n.d.), p. 308.

17. *T.W.C.* 11 (1950), p. 462.

18. *T.W.C.* 11 (1950), p. 1230. I restricted my attention to these four judgments because they raised the broadest issues insofar as application of sanctions to individual members of governmental organizations is concerned. Also relevant is the fact that some of the other Nuernberg trials seem to have dealt with conduct which does not genuinely seem to be present in Vietnam, such as criminal medical "experimentation" on the inmates of concentration camps. "The Medical Case," *T.W.C.* 2, p. 171.

An excellent distillation of doctrine drawn from all of the reported war crimes trials can be found in Morris Greenspan, *The Modern Law of Land Warfare* (Berkeley, 1959), chap. 12.

19. A useful table is provided in Anthony A. D'Amato, Harvey L. Gould, and

The IMT judgment is most helpful in considering the problem of responsibility not for traditionally recognized war crimes but rather for the more controversial category of "crimes against peace" and conspiracy to commit such crimes. These were two of the four counts upon which most of the defendants were tried; significantly, these were the only two counts for which Schacht and von Papen were prosecuted. The other two counts were the aforementioned "war crimes" and a new crime of "crimes against humanity." The last has also been the subject of much controversy, but, as indicated earlier, the justification of the various charges will not be examined here except where relevant to the principal argument.

Upon count one, conspiracy to wage crimes against peace through planning and waging aggressive war, only eight of the twenty-two were convicted: Goering, Hess, von Ribbentrop, Keitel, Rosenberg, Raeder, Jodl, and von Neurath. A similar charge was leveled at the various officials involved in the Ministries and High Command Cases, but it was ordered dropped by the tribunals.[20] The reason for this chariness to convict was the restriction of liability under this charge to those members of the German regime who were within "Hitler's inner circle of advisors" or otherwise "closely connected with the formulation of the policies which led to war."[21] As Morris Greenspan argues, to the general requirement of *mens rea*,[22] was added a requirement of actual close participation in the conspiracy.[23] This explains, then, the dismissal of conspiracy charges against all lesser figures, for by definition they could scarcely have stood within the "inner

---

Larry D. Woods, "War Crimes and Vietnam: The 'Nuremberg Defense' and the Military Service Resister," *California Law Review* 57, no. 5 (November 1969): 1055-1110, reprinted in Falk, ed., *op. cit.*, p. 414. All such later references are also taken from this table unless otherwise noted.

20. *T.W.C.* 11, pp. 482-483; 14, pp. 435-436.

21. *I.M.T.* 22, p. 547 (acquittal of Julius Streicher on charge of crimes against peace). See also the acquittal of Fritzsche, at pp. 583-584, where it is pointed out that, although head of the Home Press Division of the Reich Ministry of Popular Enlightenment and Propaganda at the time war was initiated, he did not "achieve sufficient stature to attend the planning conferences which led to aggressive war."

22. *T.W.C.* 11, pp. 488-489.

23. Greenspan, *op. cit.*, pp. 449-450 and citations therein.

circle" or else they would have been classified as "major" war criminals and tried before the IMT.[24]

The requirement of *mens rea* as to the aggressive character of German warfare also meant that the number of defendants convicted under the controversial charge of crimes against peace was minimal. At the IMT, to the eight named above who were convicted of conspiracy to commit such crimes, only three more were added—Frick, Doenitz, and Seyss-Inquart. Of the fourteen officials of the German government tried in the Ministries Case on such a count, only four were ultimately convicted.[25] Similarly the German generals tried in the High Command Case were ordered acquitted on the charge of participating in crimes against peace. The rationale for doing so should be quoted in full:

> If a defendant did not know that the planning and preparation for invasions and wars in which he was involved were concrete plans and preparations for aggressive wars and for wars otherwise in violation of international laws and treaties, then he cannot be guilty of an offense. If, however, after the policy to initiate and wage aggressive wars was formulated, a defendant came into possession of knowledge that the invasions and wars to be waged were aggressive and unlawful, then he will be criminally responsible if he, *being on the policy level, could have influenced such policy and failed to do so.*[26]

> If and as long as a member of the armed forces does not participate in the preparation, planning, initiating, or waging of aggressive war on a policy level, his war activities do not fall under the definition of crimes against peace. *It is not a person's rank or status, but his power to shape or influence the policy of his state, which is the relevant issue for determining his criminality under the charge of crimes against peace.*[27]

24. A full discussion of the conspiracy count is contained in Harold Leventhal, et al., "The Nuernberg Verdict," *Harvard Law Review* 60, no. 6 (July 1947): 863-881.

25. See *T.W.C.* 14, p. 865 for the list. Von Weizsaecker was originally convicted, but the tribunal reversed its decision. See *ibid.*, p. 950.

26. *T.W.C.* 11, pp. 488-489 (emphasis added).

27. *Ibid.*, p. 489 (emphasis added).

The defendants in question were not on the policy level and were therefore summarily acquitted.[28]

Two things should be noted. First, as mentioned above, responsibility for crimes against peace is restricted to a relatively few senior officials. For better or worse, the notion that adoption of a theory of crimes against peace or of aggressive warfare threatens to make every citizen a war criminal is incorrect. This leads to the second point, that the resolution of the key questions under counts one and two involves complex empirical judgments about the structures of power within the society in question. As we will see below in Section III, formal organization charts are entirely subordinate to empirical information regarding the *actual* distribution of influence within the German government. It is undoubtedly true that the circle of responsibility would be widened as the circle of "inner advisors" or otherwise influential associates broadened, but severe limits would still be imposed in terms of the absolute numbers of officials who could ever be held responsible for aggressive wars. The drama of just *who* would emerge in the docket would remain, but in all cases the list of candidates would be relatively small.

If the tribunals were hesitant to find guilt under the innovative and controversial charges of aggression and conspiracy to commit same, they were much less reluctant in regard to the much more traditional counts of war crimes and crimes against humanity.[29] Thus, of the

28. *Ibid.*, p. 491.
29. Technically speaking the notion of crimes against humanity is also innovative, but still much less so than conspiring to wage or actually waging an aggressive war. The terrible reason for the establishment of crimes against humanity is that the German slaughter of the Jews (and Poles, and . . .) is not cognizable within the traditional understanding of war crimes because technically these victims were not formal belligerents of the German state, and the laws of war protect only belligerents. It was not and is not a "war crime" to treat a citizen of one's own country or of one's ally iniquitously. Should one wish to protest the legality of German treatment of the Jews or South Vietnamese treatment of their own citizens, one must adopt a "crimes against humanity" analysis. Still, it is surely less controversial to do so, to decide that the wanton waste of the lives of one's nationals constitutes a crime, than to decide what constitutes "aggression." It should also be noted that the IMT limited the scope of the crime against humanity by insisting that, for conviction to ensue, such acts must be linked to the war itself; thus, German activities prior to the onset of World War II were not found cognizable (*I.M.T.* 22,

eighteen Germans accused of war crimes before the IMT, only two, Rudolph Hess, who was in a British prison throughout the war, and Fritzsche, a propagandist, were acquitted. These two were also the only two of a slightly different eighteen to escape conviction as criminals against humanity. Similarly, twelve of the fourteen officers tried under the High Command Case and eight of the ten tried in the Hostage Case were found guilty of the more traditional crimes, although, as noted above, the charges regarding crimes against peace were dismissed. In the Ministries Case, eighteen of the nineteen officials tried on counts of war crimes or crimes against humanity were convicted.

What were "war crimes"? Article 6(b) establishing the IMT defined them as

> violations of the laws or customs of war. Such violations shall include, but not be limited to, murder, ill-treatment or deportation to slave labor or for any other purpose of civilian population of or in occupied territory, murder or ill-treatment of prisoners of war or persons on the seas, killing of hostages, plunder of public or private property, wanton destruction of cities, towns, or villages, or devastation not justified by military necessity.[30]

Article 6(c) in turn defined "crimes against humanity":

> namely, murder, extermination, enslavement, deportation, and other inhumane acts committed against any civilian population, before or during the war; or persecutions on political, racial, or religious grounds in execution of or in connection with any crime within the jurisdiction of the Tribunal, whether or not in violation of the domestic law of the country where perpetrated.[31]

As pointed out above, the IMT is relatively unilluminating as to the actual standards by which guilt is to be determined. The only real

---

p. 498). For a discussion of this point and the possibly limited scope of "war crimes" in relation to Vietnam generally and to My Lai in particular, see Jordan Paust, "Legal Aspects of the My Lai Incident—A Response to Professor Rubin," *Oregon Law Review* 50, no. 2 (Winter 1971): 138-152, reprinted in Falk, ed., *op. cit.*, pp. 366ff., analyzing Article 4 of the 1949 Geneva Civilian Convention, 6 U.S.T. 3520 (1955).

30. *I.M.T.* 22, p. 471.   31. *Ibid.*, p. 496.

clue comes from its acquittal of the propagandist Fritzsche. Although
speeches he delivered indicated anti-Semitism, they "did not urge
persecution or extermination of Jews." Moreover, and significantly,
he was apparently without knowledge of the exterminations being
carried out. Indeed, there was even evidence that he had tried to sup-
press publication of the notorious *Der Sturmer*, the newspaper of
Julius Streicher, who *was* convicted and sentenced to death for crimes
against humanity for urging the destruction of the Jews. Thus, although Fritzsche's "aim was . . . to arouse popular sentiment in support of Hitler and the German war effort," this support of the regime
was analytically distinguishable from an intention "to incite the
German people to commit atrocities on conquered peoples," and so
he was acquitted.[32]

The war trials therefore stand for two linked principles: (1) Officials of governments *will* be judged on their behavior and will not
be allowed to claim either obedience to superior orders of the act-of-
state doctrine in justification. But (2), mere participation in even
the Nazi regime is not enough to label one a "war criminal." Direct
evidence of participation in the criminal acts themselves is necessary.
To be found guilty of war crimes and crimes against humanity, "there
must be a breach of some moral obligation fixed by international
law, a personal act voluntarily done with knowledge of its inherent
criminality under international law."[33] There is no strict liability for
war crimes; *mens rea* in addition to an *actus reus* is necessary.[34] The

32. *Ibid.*, pp. 584-585.   33. *T.W.C.* 11, p. 510.

34. Readers familiar with the *Yamashita* case, 327 U.S. 1 (1946), will re-
member that the Japanese general in that case was in fact subjected to what
can fairly be described as strict liability for the acts of his subordinates. Indeed
Taylor emphasizes that case in his argument that probable cause exists to believe various high military officers to be guilty of war crimes (*Nuremberg and
Vietnam: An American Tragedy* [Chicago, 1970], p. 182).

I do not rely on the *Yamashita* case in my own argument for two reasons.
First, I simply do not think the result in that case can be defended. General
Yamashita was convicted for failing to take measures to prevent commission
of war crimes even though no direct proof was offered that he ordered or even
consented to the crimes or that he had the actual power to prevent their commission. Second, insofar as I do wish to establish liability of superior officers
for the acts of their subordinates, such principles can in fact be derived from
the High Command and Hostage Cases, as will be seen below. Pragmatically
speaking, then, there is no need to embrace *Yamashita* because a more tenable

necessity to find both of these elements, indeed, raises the principal problem of this essay, for the acts themselves were most often performed by those who were in fact never tried by any major tribunal—the ordinary soldier. To find a governmental official guilty demanded the linkage of his activity to that of the final actors themselves, a most complex task.

The complexities are illustrated most clearly in the Ministries Case, dealing with civilian officials. Thus von Erdsmanndorff was acquitted in spite of the finding that he "had knowledge of the crimes against humanity committed against the Jews. . . . But a careful examination of the evidence reveals little or nothing more. It is far from enough to justify a conviction. The deputy chief of the Political Division [of the Foreign Ministry], particularly under the von Ribbentrop regime, had little or no influence. He was . . . little more than a chief clerk."[35] Similarly, Karl von Ritter, between 1940 and 1944 the liaison officer between the Foreign Ministry and the German High Command, escaped conviction on certain war crimes charges because "knowledge that a crime has been or is about to be committed is not sufficient to warrant a conviction except in those instances where an affirmative duty exists to prevent or object to a course of action."[36] It is clear that "duty" here means legal obligation and not fidelity to moral imperatives. The tribunals therefore establish no requirement of supererogatory heroism; criminal responsibility ensued only if one were directly and knowingly linked with the commission of criminal acts.

Both knowledge and actual responsibility are, of course, difficult to establish for members of complex organizations. Indeed, there is some reason to think that the convictions under the enunciated standards were the result of a fluke—that is, "the German proclivity for systematic records and the unexpectedly swift final victory, which placed files of documents in Allied hands."[37] Without such records,

---

approach exists. It is true, however, that anyone who does defend the justice of *Yamashita* must accept a concomitantly broad imputation of criminality vis-à-vis our own leadership in the Vietnam episode.

35. *T.W.C.* 14, pp. 577-578.   36. *Ibid.*, p. 625.

37. Leventhal, et al., "The Nuernberg Verdict," p. 904. Taylor stresses this point also in *Nuremberg and Vietnam*, p. 118.

convictions might have been impossible. Thus, for example, the IMT was unsympathetic to Ernst Kaltenbrunner's protestation that he lacked responsibility for the extermination of Jews, because there existed "very large numbers of orders on which his name was stamped or typed, and in a few instances, written. It is inconceivable that in matters of such importance his signature could have appeared so many times without his authority."[38] And such records were even more essential to the evaluation of lesser officials.[39]

On occasion the office held by an official could itself be probative as to whether or not certain knowledge was in fact possessed.[40] Given that all the documentation in the world, unless personally initialed, cannot actually "prove" that an official in question actually read the documents, it was stipulated that "an army commander will not ordinarily be permitted to deny knowledge of reports received at his headquarters, they being sent there for his special benefit."[41] Moreover, there is an affirmative duty to become cognizant of the actions of one's subordinates: "If he fails to require and obtain complete information, the dereliction of duty rests upon him and he is in no position to plead his own dereliction as a defense."[42] The only exception to this rule concerns "events, emergent in nature and presenting matters for original decision," where command responsibility will not be found unless the officer "approved of the action taken when it came to his knowledge."[43]

The problem of allocating responsibility becomes even more complex when we consider the distinction between line and staff officials, whether in a civilian or military context. Line officials are those who have the authority within a given structure to command others to behave in certain ways. Staff officials, on the other hand, usually have no direct authority over anyone. Their function is simply to advise, secure information, draft documents, etc. The question then arises, can staff officers be "responsible" for acts they neither directly (i.e.,

38. *I.M.T.* 22, p. 538.

39. See, for example, the remarkable documents reprinted at *T.W.C.* 11, pp. 634ff., listing, among other things, that 73 Russian soldiers, together with 1,658 Jews, had been shot in conformance to orders.

40. See, e.g., *T.W.C.* 14, pp. 697, 843.

41. *T.W.C.* 11, p. 1260.   42. *Ibid.*, p. 1271.

43. *Ibid.*, p. 1260.

physically) committed nor "ordered" others to commit? The answer is affirmative. The basic rationale is eloquently spelled out by the Tribunal in the Ministries Case:

> If the commanders of the death camps who blindly followed orders to murder the unfortunate inmates, if those who implemented or carried out the orders for the deportation of Jews to the East are properly tried, convicted, and punished; and of that we have no question whatsoever; then those who in the comparative quiet and peace of ministerial departments, aided the campaign by drafting the necessary decrees, regulations, and directives for its execution are likewise guilty.[44]

The foregoing discussion has necessarily been abstract, representing a distillation of some basic precepts from the records of four trials (out of a much larger potential sample), themselves of multiple defendants. As always it is helpful to see how they worked concretely by examining their application in a specific case. Although it would be most helpful to examine both civilian and military defendants, with line and staff duties, that would make this discussion unwieldy. Instead I shall confine my close attention to one official, and I turn now to that task.

III

Ernst von Weizsaecker was, from April 1938 through the spring of 1943, State Secretary of the German Foreign Ministry, making him second only to von Ribbentrop (who was convicted and sentenced to death by the IMT) within the formal structure having responsibility for the conduct of foreign affairs.[45] Before 1938 he had served in various capacities within the Foreign Office, which he entered in 1920. After 1943 he was German Ambassador to the Vatican. More space is devoted to him than to any other single official in the judgment in the Ministries Case, and review of his case is extremely illuminating as to the operative standards of responsibility used by that tribunal.

44. *T.W.C.* 14, pp. 645-646 (conviction of Stuckart).
45. All information about von Weizsaecker is taken from the Judgment, at *T.W.C.* 14, pp. 340-385, 463-509, 690-694, 800-801, 857, 951-959.

Von Weizsaecker was tried under seven counts—crimes against peace; participation in a common plan or conspiracy to wage aggressive war; two counts of war crimes and crimes against humanity; plunder and spoliation; slave labor; and membership in criminal organizations. As noted above, all charges were dismissed as to the count dealing with the common plan or conspiracy. Of the remainder, he was convicted only under count five, war crimes and crimes against humanity, and was acquitted on the rest. He had initially been convicted also of crimes against peace, but this was reversed upon petitioning the tribunal for review.

The importance of documentary evidence was mentioned above; although usually this provided the specific means of connecting given individuals to particular events, at least in von Weizsaecker's case it also established the evidence by which he could be acquitted, for his defense essentially turned on his lack of affirmative participation in the creation and execution of the aggressive German policies. Documentary evidence existed that could demonstrate "not only that he was not engaged in planning or preparing an aggressive war, but that he was averse to it and that he expressed no thought that in the long run it would be successful, but on the contrary that it would involve disaster to Germany."[46] Thus even the second-ranking officer of the Foreign Ministry could escape liability for the general policies and acts of his Government if evidence existed as to his internal opposition (within the bureaucracy, though not publicly expressed) to them.

Such internal opposition is not enough to mandate exculpation if the individual in question otherwise "aided or abetted or took a consenting part"[47] in the activities under examination, but it is clear from the treatment of von Weizsaecker that stricter standards as to the meaning of such aid or consent were used if evidence of opposition were available than if there were none.[48] Perhaps the most interest-

46. *Ibid.*, p. 346.
47. *Ibid.*, p. 349.
48. See especially the memorandum reversing the initial finding of guilt under count one, *ibid.*, pp. 954-955. Originally the tribunal had held that, in relation to the invasion of Czechoslovakia, alone of the number of individual instances of aggressive war analyzed, he "was not a mere bystander," but instead an affirmative actor (*ibid.*, p. 354).

ing specific example of the intricate approach taken by the Tribunal is in regard to von Weizsaecker's responsibility for the invasion of Poland:

> Von Weizsaecker had no part in the plan for Polish aggression; he was not in the confidence of either Hitler or von Ribbentrop. While his position was one of prominence and he was one of the principal cogs in the machinery which dealt with foreign policy, nevertheless as a rule, he was an implementor and not an originator. He could oppose and object, but he could not override. Therefore, we seek to ascertain what he did and whether he did all that lay in his power to frustrate a policy which outwardly he appeared to support. *If in fact he so acted, we are not interested in his formal, official declarations, instructions, or interviews with foreign diplomats.*[49]

Thus although the tribunal, considering von Weizsaecker's culpability for the invasion of the Low Countries, agreed that in fact his statements to the Belgian ambassador were "deceptive" in regard to German intentions and admitted that "were we to judge him only by these things alone we would be compelled to the conclusion that he was consciously, even though unwillingly, participating in the plans,"[50] he is still acquitted. The panel notes that "in determining matters of this kind we may not substitute the calm, undisturbed judgment derived from after knowledge, wholly divorced from the strain and emotions of the event, for that of the man who was in the midst of things, distracted by the impact of the conflagration and torn by conflicting emotions and his traditional feelings of nationality."[51] It is enough that von Weizsaecker opposed these policies, an opposition which eventuated in his playing "a real part in the continuous underground opposition to and plots against Hitler."[52] It is fair to say that a *de minimis* test of aiding and abetting was adopted, whereby less than "substantial"[53] participation in the execution of German invasions was treated as no participation at all.

There was no disputing the charge that von Weizsaecker was in

49. *Ibid.*, p. 356 (emphasis added).
50. *Ibid.*, p. 378.
51. *Id.*   52. *Id.*   53. *Ibid.*, p. 380.

fact aware of the aggressive nature of the German actions.[54] What was lacking was affirmative participation. It was, however, also suggested that, knowing of their aggressive character, he had an affirmative obligation to go beyond internal opposition to actual attempts at sabotage. Thus it was asked why he did not inform the Russian ambassador of Hitler's plans against his country in 1941. The tribunal dismisses this argument. After first pointing to the danger to which he would have had to expose himself, the panel said it was enough that he had opposed the invasion within the Foreign Ministry. But it then goes on to make a separate argument, for it notes that such betrayal of his country would not in fact have changed Hitler's policy, but would have led only to greater German losses because of Soviet preparations.

> The prosecution insists, however, that there is criminality in his assertion that he did not desire the defeat of his own country. The answer is: Who does? One may quarrel with, and oppose to the point of violence and assassination, a tyrant whose programs mean the ruin of one's country. But the time has not yet arrived when any man would view with satisfaction the ruin of his own people and the loss of its young manhood. To apply any other standard of conduct is to set up a test that has never yet been suggested as proper, and which, assuredly, we are not prepared to accept as either wise or good.[55]

Undoubtedly some of the relative generosity shown von Weizsaecker is to be explained by a more general reservation as to the legitimacy of the alleged crime of participation in aggressive war. Although the tribunal followed the IMT in upholding the validity of that charge under international law, it was reluctant to convict without overwhelming evidence of both knowledge and participation, and it was concomitantly willing to accept counterevidence of the type used so successfully by von Weizsaecker. What is especially remarkable is its willingness to minimize the importance of formal diplomatic activity. The tribunal was, however, much less generous to the defendant in regard to more traditional crimes of war.

54. See, e.g., *ibid.*, p. 382.   55. *Ibid.*, p. 383.

In its initial discussion of the responsibility of von Weizsaecker for the extermination of the Jews, the tribunal repeats the central theme that responsibility attaches only where the accused individual occupies a position within the governmental structure of actual authority to affect or implement policy. Because the Foreign Office had no jurisdiction, for example, over the activities of the Einsatzgruppen operations in the Eastern European countries, there was no responsibility, even though there was knowledge of them.[56] It is perhaps true that no "decent man could continue to hold office under a regime which carried out planned and wholesale barbarities of this kind," but indecency is not a crime.[57]

In other aspects relating to treatment of the Jews, however, the Foreign Office had not only knowledge but also authority, and here the decision as to criminality would be different. Here, too, von Weizsaecker attempted to argue that minimal participation should be negated by the fact that he opposed what was being done. Indeed, he argued that he remained in office until 1 May 1943 for two central reasons: he could continue to plan some meaningful role in the underground opposition to Hitler by retaining access to important information and distributing such information, and he "might be in a position to initiate or aid in attempts to negotiate peace." The tribunal specifically stated that it believed his claims, but went on to note also that, whatever force they might have in mitigating punishment, they cannot be a defense to charges of crimes of war or crimes against humanity. "One cannot give consent to or implement the commission of murder because by so doing he hopes eventually to be able to rid society of the chief murderer. The first is a crime of imminent actuality while the second is but a future hope."[58] Thus the State Secretary was under an affirmative obligation to object, upon inquiry by the SS as to the Foreign Office's opinions in regard to the treatment of Jews. Failure to object was grounds for being found guilty, as von Weizsaecker here was. This was the sole instance where he was in fact convicted, and for this he received a sentence of seven years.[59]

56. *Ibid.*, p. 472.   57. *Id.*   58. *Ibid.*, pp. 497-498.

59. *Ibid.*, pp. 498, 866. It should be noted that Judge Powers filed a sharp dissent to the judgment of his two colleagues that guilt attached even in this instance (*ibid.*, pp. 910-913).

IV

It is time now to turn from Nuernberg to Vietnam. What inferences
can we draw from the preceding material? What would be necessary
were we to decide to try individual high officials of the American
government, past or present, for war crimes which have undoubtedly
taken place as part of the Vietnam War?[60]

At least two distinct questions are raised by suggestions for holding
war crimes trials. The first is deceptively simple: taking the Nuernberg principles sketched above as given, what kinds of evidence would
be needed in order to convict officials of war crimes?[61] The second
question is more obviously complex: given the extreme unlikelihood
that trials for war crimes will in fact be held under official auspices,
either domestically or internationally, what alternatives are open to
the lay citizenry who remain convinced not only that crimes have
occurred, but also that there may be criminals to whom can be allocated responsibility? The first question can be answered from within
the accepted legal tradition. The second, however, involves what
would frankly be an exercise of extralegal judgment, an attempt to
make at least quasi-legal findings (i.e., that given individuals are
"war criminals") without legal authority to do so. The second question

---

It is also true that, regarding the deportation of Hungarian Jews, von
Weizsaecker's linkage was found "so slight and insignificant" that he was
acquitted, so even here some kind of *de minimis* test remained (*ibid.*, pp. 499,
507, 508, 526).

60. For evidence as to the commission of both conventional war crimes as
well as the crime of aggressive war, see the essays collected in Falk, *op. cit.*,
as well as, e.g., Richard A. Falk, Gabriel Kolko, and Robert Jay Lifton, eds.,
Crimes of War (New York, 1971). See also the review by Neil Sheehan, "Should
We Have War Crimes Trials?" *The New York Times Book Review*, 28 March
1971, p. 1, reviewing 33 books alleging the commission of war crimes. There
has also been testimony by ex-servicemen themselves as to war crimes in Vietnam. See, e.g., material introduced into the *Congressional Record* by Senator
Hatfield on 6-7 April 1971, pp. E2825-2900, 2903-2936.

61. Again it should be emphasized that one may not want to take the
Nuernberg principles as given, especially insofar as the trials simply ignored
the issue of civilian bombing by refusing to charge any defendant for such
action (presumably because any defendant would have been able to charge
tu quoque in regard to the Allied bombing). See Taylor, *Nuremberg and Vietnam*, pp. 140-145. See also Taylor, "Defining War Crimes," *The New York Times*,
11 January 1973, p. 39, referring specifically to the bombing of Hanoi.

is not logically entailed by the principal topic of this essay—theories of responsibility. It is, however, linked to any affirmative response to the question of whether viable standards of responsibility exist, for we are then faced with the dilemma of a positive legal system which refuses to apply "the law." What response is then open to the citizen who sees a conflict not between law and morality, but rather between law and a particular legal structure which refuses enforcement?

As to the first question it is clear from the discussion above how dependent the Nuernberg trials were on captured documents. The judgments were careful to document the connections between given officials and the acts for which they were accused of responsibility; there was a minimum of reliance on purely formal analysis of responsibility within governmental organizations. Such documents were available for two separate reasons. The first was, of course, the fortuitous capture of the papers of the regime by the victorious Allies. But the second reason is perhaps of greater relevance insofar as application of the Nuernberg precedents to American officials is concerned, and that is simply that the most essential fact about the Nazi regime was that it consciously articulated and executed such policies as the Holocaust or the brutal murders of prisoners of war and hostages. Having consciously adopted the policies, the regime took great care to measure their enforcement through the preparation of copious reports, memoranda, etc. Individuals in turn proved their fidelity to the regime by documenting their own acquiescence in its orders.[62]

Not even the most bitter critic of American policy would suggest that it has been the result of clearly articulated, clearly ordered, and clearly executed desires to flaunt international law and morality in the same way as was true of Germany. Thus, even if American documents were capable of being subpoenaed or captured, it is doubtful that evidence similar to that introduced at Nuernberg would be found. The most maddening characteristic of officials of the American government, to their critics, is their *denial* of the carnage that has taken place in Vietnam, rather than their exhaltation of the slaughter in the name of the American *volk*.

62. See Hannah Arendt, *Eichmann in Jerusalem* (New York, revised edition, 1965), chap. 8: "Duties of a Law-Abiding Citizen."

It is also important to distinguish clearly problems attendant on trying civilian officials from those present regarding military officers. Thus, concerning the latter, it is quite possible, as Taylor and others have suggested,[63] that the very failure to investigate charges of war crimes that have been leveled is itself criminal under the standards articulated in the High Command Case. Without accepting the scope of *Yamashita*, one can still argue that military commanders are obliged to organize the armed forces so as to maximize the likelihood of exercizing meaningful discipline over the troops and preventing the commission of criminal acts. Insofar as evidence does exist that the American command in Vietnam breached his duty, there would seem to be few purely legal problems involved in trying officers for at least some of the crimes committed there.[64]

The judgments are much murkier, however, regarding the responsibilities of civilian officials to assure that they will be provided with accurate information, on pain of liability should they not seek such data. Without such evidence as was available at Nuernberg, it is tempting to adopt formalist theories of government to assume without more that the occupant of a given office is automatically a "war criminal" because an organization chart puts him in formal control of given subordinates. But this begs the question of the knowledge by superiors of criminal action, the ease with which accurate information might have been available, or the relationship between formal authority and actual power.

What constitutes acquiescence in criminal activity? For example, the Department of Defense rightly notes that Americans in Vietnam received formal instruction in the rights granted by the Geneva Convention.[65] In spite of all the doubts one might have about the actual

63. Taylor, *Nuremberg and Vietnam*, pp. 123-182; see also "Playboy Interview: Anthony Herbert," *Playboy* (July 1972): 59ff., concerning the experiences of an Army colonel who attempted to inform superiors about the commission of war crimes.

64. Seymour Hersch, *Coverup* (New York, 1972), documents the suppression by American officials of information concerning the crimes committed at My Lai. His principal source of information is the still-secret Peers Report, based on investigations conducted by the Army itself.

65. Hersch, *op. cit.*, pp. 40-41.

fidelity to that Convention or to orders to obey it, how does one establish the culpability of high governmental officials for breaches of the Convention by subordinates if those officials have in fact issued such orders? Is it enough simply to say that they were perfunctory, hypocritical, self-deluded, etc.?

The tribunals were particularly stringent about finding guilt for participation in the crime of aggressive war. Insofar as some critics of the Vietnam War emphasize its aggressive character (i.e., on the part of the American government), those critics would face what seems to be an insurmountable problem of proving actual knowledge of the aggressive character of American participation, in addition to the difficulty of selecting out those officials who actively brought about the war. Indeed, for a conspiracy charge to be sustained,[66] one would, among other things, have to identify the "inner circles" of the Kennedy and Johnson Administrations. Whatever one might think of the "decency" of ex-Vice President Humphrey, for example, in serving the Johnson Administration's foreign policy, it would seem impossible, on the basis of currently available information, to suggest seriously that he is a "war criminal," for he does not seem to have been in any strong sense a member of the "inner circle." He is culpable only if we adopt what Nuernberg specifically rejected—the obligation to resign from an administration engaging in criminal activity.[67]

66. See Noam Chomsky, "The Rule of Force in International Affairs," *Yale Law Journal* 80, no. 7 (June 1971) (review of Taylor): 1459 n. 14.

67. Though see Richard A. Falk, "Son My: War Crimes and Individual Responsibility," in Falk, ed., *The Vietnam War and International Law* 3, pp. 338-339, where he quotes a passage from the Tokyo judgment which *does* suggest an affirmative duty to resign: "If [a Cabinet member] has knowledge of ill-treatment, but elects to remain in the Cabinet thereby continuing to participate in its collective responsibility for protection of prisoners, he willingly assumes responsibility for any ill-treatment in the future." Falk goes on to argue that it is therefore now part of the law of war that "A leader must take affirmative acts to prevent war crimes or dissociate himself from the government. If he fails to do one or the other, then by the very act of remaining in a government of a state guilty of war crimes, he becomes a war criminal" (*ibid.*, p. 339). I do not think that an analysis of the Nuernberg judgments supports this statement. (One way of rationalizing the quoted statement with the analysis in the text is to argue that by its terms the Tokyo rule operates *only* where there is a Cabinet which does operate on a theoretical basis of collective responsibility. Where that is not the case, as it certainly is not in this country, then there would be no duty to resign.)

In summary, then, although it might be disputed whether or not
the lack of copious documentary evidence raises a "well-nigh insuperable" obstacle to the holding of American war crimes trials,[68] it can
scarcely be disputed that severe problems are raised if we wish to
adhere to the standards set at Nuernberg. It is arguable, though,
that the problems are of differential severity in regard to the specific
kinds of war crimes under discussion. Thus convictions for waging
aggressive war *do* depend on specific information relating to both
knowledge and actual power in a way that does not seem to be the
case for more traditional war crimes. Critics of the war who focus
more on the means with which it has been fought rather than its
allegedly aggressive character would seem to have a slightly easier
task in terms of proving culpability. As noted above, one's office
within an organization, even if not determinative as to actual responsibility, nevertheless may properly raise a presumption of some degree of responsibility. Is it unfair, then, to expect certain officials to
come forward with evidence that they did *not* actively join in the
commission of criminal policies? That is, if one (a) proves that a
criminal pattern of activity developed in the conduct of the war, and
(b) shows that the institutional roles filled by the men in question
have at least formal responsibility for the policies in question, then
a prima facie case is established, and it is reasonable to expect the
individuals to demonstrate that the case fails.

Moreover, it is worth mentioning that information, even if less reliable than the captured German documents, *is* available about the
policy-making apparatus in charge of the war. There are not only
the Pentagon Papers, but also such studies as David Halberstam's
The Best and the Brightest; it is possible, as well, that more officials
of the relevant administrations will feel it wise or necessary to publish accounts of how *they*, at least, were never so foolish as Walt
Rostow, and thus illuminate further, even if self-servingly, the param-
eters of power.

68. Taylor, *op. cit.*, p. 118. It is this specific assertion that Chomsky, *op. cit.*,
disputes. Like Richard Falk, "Nuremberg: Past, Present, and Future," *Yale Law
Journal* 80, no. 7 (June 1971) (review of Taylor): 1501-1528, Chomsky believes that the Pentagon Papers provide a sufficient evidentiary base from which
to determine guilt or innocence of war crimes.

But, of course, official trials are not going to be held, and discussion about procedures that might be used at such trials is academic. If law is indeed only that which courts are prepared to enforce, then the status of the law of war is weak. Yet, as noted above, it is possible to argue that law has an existence independent of the willingness of the state to enforce it, and that it is fruitful to discuss what alternatives to official trials might exist for establishing who, if anyone, bears blame for illegalities attached to the Vietnam War. Two general alternatives suggest themselves. One is the establishment by inevitably self-appointed groups or individuals of a citizens' tribunal which would consider the guilt of named officials and publish its assessments.[69] A second alternative would be the preparation by individual scholars of articles, to be published perhaps in law reviews, as to the guilt or innocence of named individuals under the applicable precedents. One article might be on Lyndon Johnson, another on McGeorge Bundy, a third on Henry Kissinger, etc.

The problems with both alternatives, of course, are obvious. They raise spectres of at best a "left-wing McCarthyism" and at worst a peculiarly academic version of lynch law. It is one thing to have such extralegal tribunals or individuals consider the question of whether or not the United States, as a reified entity, committed crimes. The affirmative answer which would be forthcoming could be used to support the idea that this country has an obligation, in spite of the problems noted in section one above, to provide reparations to the North and South Vietnamese victimized by its criminal activities. But

69. See, e.g., Falk, *op. cit.*, pp. 344-345 n. 66, who suggests "a national board of legal experts" to review violations of the laws of war in Vietnam. On the other hand, Falk in this article specifically rejects the preparation by such a board of criminal indictments against named individuals, on the grounds that this would be "scapegoating" and an attempt to relinquish a more widely shared responsibility for the war. However, see Falk's review of Taylor, *op. cit.* n. 67, p. 1503, where he speaks of "putative 'war criminals' being rewarded with such jobs as the presidency of the World Bank, the presidency of the Ford Foundation, the editorship of Foreign Affairs, and high-salaried professorships at leading American institutions of learning." Given that a minimally aware reader can identify Robert McNamara, McGeorge Bundy, William Bundy, and Walt W. Rostow, it appears that Falk may now be more receptive to reviewing the actions of named public officials.

it is entirely different to discuss the responsibility of named individuals—or so the argument would run.

It should immediately be noted that the objection to extralegal proceedings cannot necessarily take the form that they would deny "due process" to the affected individuals, for it is easy to conceive of a citizens' tribunal which would follow impeccably every evidentiary rule and other requirement perceived as necessary to "due process." The objection to such proceedings must take a more fundamental form—that it is always illegitimate for private citizens to try to enforce the law in the face of refusals by the State to do so. If one's sole objection to Senator McCarthy is that he refused to depend on the authoritative legal institutions of the society to repress those accused of communist sympathies, instead of pointing to the ruthless disregard of due process in the procedures by which he determined the culpability of his victims, then there is in truth no answer to the charge of "left-wing McCarthyism." I would argue, however, that to focus only on the unwillingness to trust the existing formal institutions of the society to enforce the law is to beg the question of *why* those institutions are necessarily the only ones that can legitimately, in anything more than a formal sense, maintain legal norms by using them as a source of judgment concerning the conduct of members of the society.

And, it must be stressed, recourse to extralegal determination of "guilt" is entirely separate, analytically, from recourse to similar determinations of "punishment." One can oppose, that is, the actions of a lynch mob, without necessarily denying the accuracy of their perception that the individual in question is "in fact" guilty of the crime for which he is accused, even though the formal system, for given reasons, is incapable of declaring him guilty.[70]

The most appalling aspect of America's participation in the Vietnam War, aside from the slaughter itself, has been the refusal to

70. For those bothered by this last sentence, I ask them to consider their own reactions to the acquittals of southern whites in the early 1960's for the murder of civil rights workers and leaders like Medgar Evers, or more recent acquittals of policemen for charges linked to the suppression of black militants. Even if one would not wish to "punish" the acquitted assassin of Evers, is it *necessarily* wrong to regard him as factually guilty and therefore deserving of moral condemnation and stigmatization?

take seriously the allegations of war criminality which have been put forth. The obvious reason for this reluctance is that to take the Nuernberg principles seriously is to admit the reality of criminal responsibility on the part of high officials. At the same time even some critics who would accept the notion that criminal activities have occurred would still attribute these activities (outcomes) to the mechanisms of impersonal institutions. As argued at the beginning of this essay, there are good reasons for doing so.

Yet Daniel Ellsberg is surely right to argue that governmental officials should be called to account for their deeds, if that is at all possible. To accept without restriction the view of government as articulated by Murray Edelman is to descend further into a completely Kafkaesque world of institutions without actors, a mad kind of world where individual activities (though not "decisions") culminate in a world that no one desires and for which no one is responsible. To reject without question Edelman's view, on the other hand, is to fall just as surely into the opposite trap of believing that great events in fact can be traced to great individuals, whether members of a conspiracy or "dictators." Unfortunately, it seems likely that those who are sympathetic to extralegal tribunals are too ready to assign individual responsibility to all officials of the American government. But it is just as likely that those who automatically condemn extralegal judgment are all too generous to American policy-makers in rejecting either the criminal nature of at least aspects of the war or the responsibility of discrete human beings for the consequences of their actions.

Given the intractable dilemma, however, it is still necessary to choose a lesser evil, and I submit that at this time the lesser evil is to engage in analysis of the behavior of named individuals, with a concomitant willingness to announce that there is, or is not, "probable cause" to believe that they are war criminals. Such discussion would at the very least contribute to the sorely needed analysis of the notion of individual responsibility for the outcomes of complex organizations. If one ultimately decides that Edelman (and Tolstoy and Kafka) are correct, then at least that decision will not be made by default. If it *can* be determined to what extent responsibility is allocable, then the principles developed will have wide application, for increasingly all significant social activity takes place through the aegis of complex organizations.

As to the individuals in question, there is the blunt fact that they are members of the dominant social and political elites of this country. McGeorge Bundy, Richard Nixon, and Henry Kissinger can handily defend themselves against the charges of being war criminals in ways that an ordinary citizen could not. Though any injustice done to an individual is a cause for concern, there is greater reason to be concerned by the social consequences of not making such inquiries. Moreover, to move beyond a mere utilitarian justification, there remains, though now out of fashion, a view of the world which emphasizes our rootedness in a moral order which in itself generates demands that wrongdoers be identified and punished, even if only through stigmatization, in order to restore a moral harmony which is dislocated when injustice of the nature present in Vietnam occurs.[71]

71. See Yosal Rogat, *The Eichmann Trial and the Rule of Law* (Santa Barbara, 1961), p. 22; Arendt, *op. cit.*, pp. 278-279.

Persons who vigorously oppose the Vietnam War sometimes rely heavily, if not exclusively, upon Nuremberg as the justification for their opposition. They take Nuremberg to be relevant, if not decisive, in two respects: as defining the substantive principles by which the behavior of the United States is to be adjudged; and as enumerating the principles of responsibility by which the behavior of individual citizens of the United States is to be governed.

Much has been written about the former of these two topics, and there is no shortage of literature devoted to the question of whether and by what means the United States is guilty of having committed crimes against peace, war crimes, and crimes against humanity in Vietnam. Substantially less has been written about the principles of individual responsibility, and there is a good deal of genuine confusion in this area.

It is this latter issue to which I address myself, and to certain questions and problems that are raised by and about Nuremberg. More specifically, in what follows I try to answer three basic questions: (1) What were the principles of individual responsibility that were established at Nuremberg? (2) How might one argue that these principles justify a refusal to accept induction into the United States armed forces? (3) What are the strengths and weaknesses of basing such a refusal upon an appeal to Nuremberg?

In the course of attempting to answer these questions, I hope also to explain why there is so much confusion about the principles of individual responsibility that were established at Nuremberg and why there is so much uncertainty about the applicability of these principles to Americans. There is, I believe, a genuine phenomenon here that needs explaining. For on the one hand, appeals to Nuremberg are fairly regularly put forward as a justification—if not the central justification—for a wide variety of antiwar activities: the refusal to train Green Berets in medical techniques; the refusal of soldiers to serve in Vietnam; the refusal to accept induction into the armed forces; the destruction of draft cards; the destruction of draft board records; and the destruction of draft board offices. On the other hand, for a variety of reasons that are seldom if ever elucidated, appeals to Nuremberg are almost never taken seriously by those of the Establishment—be it the judiciary, the rest of the government, or most of those who applaud or criticize the activities of the war-opposers. There has been little if any discussion emanating from either the respectable hawks or doves as to why the appeals to Nuremberg are not apt. There has been virtually no explanation offered to those who cite Nuremberg as to why or where they are mistaken. The typical attitude—with the possible exception of the trial of Captain Levy[1]—is that such appeals are too silly, too wrong-headed, too inappropriate to deserve comment, let alone refutation.

It is, of course, easy to see some of the reasons why this is so. Those who support the war, and even many who oppose it, are not likely to possess the objectivity that would lead them to regard their own actions in such a sinister light. Nonetheless, over and above this sort of explanation, a genuine area of confusion and bewilderment about the applicability of Nuremberg does still remain. And it is this that I think I can, at least in part, account for.

Finally, it should be made quite clear at the outset that I assume throughout my analysis, what does seem to me to be the case, that the United States has committed and is still committing crimes against peace, war crimes, and crimes against humanity in Vietnam.

I

The rules and principles that were to govern the proceedings of the Tribunal that sat at Nuremberg were laid down in the Charter of the

---

1. See, for one report, Andrew Kopkind, "Captain Levy I—Doctor's Plot," in Noam Chomsky et al., *Trials of the Resistance* (New York, 1970), pp. 25-26.

International Military Tribunal, a document prepared in 1945 by France, Great Britain, Russia, and the United States. For present purposes four articles of the Charter are important, Articles Six, Seven, Eight, and Ten. These articles set forth principles of two different kinds: first, there are those principles that define various substantive offenses or crimes for which the perpetrators are to be held responsible; and second, there are the principles that deal with the conditions of individual responsibility. Thus, Article Six of the Charter speaks to both kinds of issues. It begins by announcing:

> The following acts, or any of these, are crimes coming within jurisdiction of the Tribunal for which there shall be individual responsibility.
>
> (a) Crimes Against Peace: namely, planning, preparation, initiation or waging of a war of aggression, or a war in violation of international treaties, agreements or assurances, or participation in a common plan or conspiracy for the accomplishment of any of the foregoing.
>
> (b) War Crimes: namely, violations of the laws or customs of war. Such *violations* shall include, but not be limited to, murder, ill-treatment or deportation to slave labor or for any other purpose of civilian population of or in occupied territory, murder or ill-treatment of prisoners of war or persons on the seas, killing of hostages, plunder of public property, wanton destruction of cities, towns or villages, or devastation not justified by military necessity.
>
> (c) Crimes Against Humanity: namely, murder, extermination, enslavement, deportation, and other inhuman acts committed against any civilian population, before or during the war, or persecutions on political, racial or religious grounds in execution of or in connection with any crime within the jurisdiction of the Tribunal, whether or not in violation of the domestic law of the country where perpetrated.[2]

The general principle of individual responsibility is never formulated explicitly. Article Six simply announces that there "shall be indi-

2. "Charter of the International Military Tribunal," *Trial of the Major War Criminals Before the International Military Tribunal* (Washington, D.C., 1947), I, 11.

vidual responsibility" for anyone who commits any of the enumerated crimes. But the conditions of individual responsibility are, nonetheless, clarified in the remainder of Article Six and in Articles Seven, Eight, and Ten, where certain special conditions of liability and certain specific excuses are dealt with. The remaining portion of Article Six and Article Ten are concerned with principles of vicarious or extended liability. Article Six establishes this liability in respect to participation in a common plan or conspiracy. "Leaders, organizers, instigators and accomplices participating in the formulation or execution of a common plan or conspiracy to commit any of the foregoing crimes are responsible for all acts performed by any persons in execution of such plan."[3] The language is quite sweeping, and a number of the key terms, e.g., "common plan" or "conspiracy," are left undefined. Conspiring to do certain things is itself a crime. And the principle is a principle of vicarious liability in that it holds any member of a conspiracy liable for any and all of the acts committed by other members of the conspiracy. Regrettably, this principle is not very different from what we would find in the criminal law of most Anglo-American jurisdictions.

Article Ten formulates a less familiar principle of responsibility, in which responsibility is derived from membership in a group. Article Nine had provided that the jurisdiction of the Tribunal would extend to a determination of whether various groups were or were not criminal groups. Article Ten then provides that "In cases where a group or organization is declared criminal by the Tribunal, the competent national authority of any signatory shall have the right to bring individuals to trial for membership therein before national, military, or occupation courts. In any such case the criminal nature of the group or organization is considered proved and shall not be questioned."[4] In other words, if a group has been found by the Tribunal to have been criminal, then membership in the group at some earlier time is itself a separate and distinct offense. This clearly has the ring of ex post facto legislation and adjudication to it. It also adopts the principle that action of a very minimal sort and a sort not typically criminal—becoming a member of some group—is sufficient to render one culpable.

3. *Ibid.*
4. *Ibid.*, p. 12.

Articles Seven and Eight are concerned with certain possible defenses conceivably open to individuals otherwise guilty of committing
the actions made criminal by Article Six. In both cases the purport of
the article is to abolish the potential defense.

Article Seven deals with the less interesting and persuasive of the
two defenses, the so-called Act of State Doctrine. In simplest form the
Doctrine is the embodiment of the notion that the head of a state is
under no circumstances to be subjected to criminal liability by any
other country or groups of countries. Article Seven of the Charter dismisses this doctrine quite peremptorily. "The official position of defendants, whether as Heads of State or responsible officials in Government departments, shall not be considered as freeing them from
responsibility or mitigating punishment."[5]

It is difficult, I think, for us to get very excited about the elimination
of this defense—indeed, it is not terribly easy to see how or why the
Act of State Doctrine would ever get formulated in the first place.
What seems to be involved is an excessive, metaphysical preoccupation with the nature and sanctity of the nation-state. Not surprisingly,
perhaps, the importance of the Act of State Doctrine was championed
by the government of the United States in 1919. At that time the argument for the doctrine was articulated this way: "This [the Act of State
Doctrine] does not mean that the head of the State, whether he is
called emperor, king, or chief executive, is not responsible for breaches
of the law, but that he is responsible not to the judicial but to the
political authority of his country. His act may and does bind his country and render it responsible for the acts which he has committed in
its name, and its behalf, or under cover of its authority; but he is, and
it is submitted that he should be, only responsible to his country, as
otherwise to hold would be to subject to foreign countries, a chief
executive, thus withdrawing him from the laws of his country, even
its organic law, to which he owes obedience, and subordinating him
to foreign jurisdictions to which neither he nor his country owes allegiance or obedience, thus denying the very conception of sovereignty."[6]

5. *Ibid.*
6. "Report of the Committee on Responsibilities," *Carnegie Endowment for
International Peace*, Pamphlet No. 32 (1919), pp. 65-66. Quoted in Wilbourn
E. Benton and George Grimm, *Nuremberg: German Views of the War Trials*
(Dallas, 1955), p. 20.

The same point was put more tersely by one of the attorneys for the Nuremberg defendants, Dr. Herman Jahrreiss: the leaders of Germany ought not, he argued, to be prosecuted for the fact that the German state waged aggressive war, because individual responsibility in such circumstances simply "cannot take place as long as the sovereignty of states is the organizational basic principle of interstate order."[7] This is a strange doctrine indeed. If anyone is properly to be held responsible for impermissible behavior in respect to war, it ought surely to be that person or those persons who had the most to do with bringing it about that that impermissible behavior took place.

The second, more interesting, and clearly more relevant defense is that based upon the plea of superior orders. Intuitively, the claim that someone who acted only when ordered to do so should be excused from criminal liability strikes a responsive chord. It is at least as initially attractive as the Act of State Doctrine is initially implausible. The Charter took the hard line in respect to the problem of superior orders: "The fact that the defendant acted pursuant to order of his government or of a superior shall not free him from responsibility, but may be considered in mitigation of punishment if the Tribunal determined that justice so required."[8] I shall return later for a more detailed examination of this crucial provision.

If we look just at the language of the relevant provisions of the Charter a fairly simple, but also intimidating, scheme of responsibility is established. (1) Persons who commit any of the enumerated crimes against peace, war crimes, or crimes against humanity, including the waging of aggressive war, are to be held individually responsible for their actions. (2) Persons who are members of a common plan or conspiracy to commit any of the crimes specified are liable for the acts performed by any other members of the conspiracy or plan. (3) Persons who are members of groups declared to be criminal are liable to criminal punishment for having been members of such groups. (4) The Act of State Doctrine is irrelevant to questions of liability and punishment. (5) The plea of superior orders is relevant to questions of punishment but not to questions of responsibility. Taken together, these principles surely cast a very wide and fine net

7. Quoted in Benton and Grimm, *Nuremberg*, p. 53.
8. *Trial of the Major War Criminals*, I, 12.

of responsibility. Given, for example, our assumption that the United States is involved in the commission of crimes against peace, war crimes, and crimes against humanity, all members of the armed forces as well as countless civilians appear to come within these principles of responsibility. And the principles of the responsibility of coconspirators and the criminality of group membership appear to extend the range still further. If one were to read only the Charter of the International Military Tribunal, it is hard to see how anyone could fail to talk about Nuremberg very, very seriously.

But part of the problem and much of the confusion about what Nuremberg means arises, I think, from the fact that there is more to Nuremberg than the Charter. There is also the judgment of the Tribunal that sat at Nuremberg, adjudged the guilt and innocence of the individual defendants there, and interpreted and refined the principles of responsibility enunciated in the Charter. Almost without exception, the interpretations of the Charter had the effect of contracting substantially the ambit of liability ostensibly adumbrated by the Charter. In some respects, there are really two Nurembergs: the principles of the Nuremberg Charter and the principles of the judgment of the Tribunal.

The Tribunal overtly modified the principles of the Charter in two significant respects. In the first place, the Tribunal only half accepted the Charter's rejection of the plea of superior orders. It did so by adding some sort of a defense of duress. Here is what the Tribunal said: "It was . . . submitted on behalf of most of these defendants that in doing what they did they were acting under the orders of Hitler, and therefore cannot be held responsible for the acts committed by them in carrying out these orders. . . . The provisions of . . . Article [Eight] are in conformity with the law of all nations. That a soldier was ordered to kill or torture in violation of the international law of war has never been recognized as a defence to such acts of brutality, though, as the Charter here provides, the order may be urged in mitigation of the punishment. The true test, which is found in varying degrees in the criminal law of most nations, is not the existence of the order, but whether moral choice was in fact possible."[9]

9. "Judgment of the International Military Tribunal," *Trial of the Major War Criminals*, I, 223-224.

It is difficult to imagine a more obscure way of characterizing the nature of the defense that, the Tribunal was prepared to allow, and I will return shortly to a more careful examination of what this means. For the time being, however, it is sufficient simply to note that a substantial alteration of the general schema of liability was effected.

The second explicit modification concerned the range of the conspiracy doctrine and its attendant principle of vicarious liability. For reasons that are not relevant here, the Tribunal read the Charter as creating a separate crime of conspiracy only in respect to the commission of crimes against peace. It refused, that is, to recognize as crimes conspiracies to commit crimes of war or crimes against humanity.[10]

It is clear, I think, that these two interpretations or modifications of the principles of individual responsibility laid down in the Charter do constitute reasonably major changes in the overall schema. Thus the fact that there is this disparity between the Charter and the judgment of the Tribunal does account in part for the confusion that attends discussions of what Nuremberg was all about. But it hardly begins to explain the core of uncertainty that is embedded in all such inquiries. It does not make clear why some persons see these principles as having momentous consequences for their own behavior while other persons regard them as manifestly irrelevant—even, it must be recalled, when both agree generally upon the character of the United States' wrongdoing in Vietnam. We must, therefore, look beyond the language of both the Charter and the Tribunal, to what was done, as well as to what was said.

II

The most significant source of difficulty is, I think, the question of the meaning that is to be derived from either set of principles (those of the Charter or those of the judgment of the Tribunal) as applied to particular cases. This can best be brought out, I believe, by concentrating reasonably carefully upon one of the many kinds of cases in which disagreements about the relevance of Nuremberg are apt to arise. The case that I propose to focus upon is that intermediate case of the person who is ordered to report for induction into the armed

10. *Ibid.*, p. 226.

forces.[11] Of what relevance to him are the Nuremberg principles of
responsibility when he is confronted with the decision whether to
accept or to refuse induction?[12]

Let us begin by asking what the arguments would be for accepting
induction. In a general way, the train of discourse might well go something like this:

"In the first place, the law requires this person to accept induction,
and in a democracy like the United States, that by itself is a good and
sufficient reason for doing that which is required.

"Moreover, even if it is true that the United States is committing all
of the crimes stipulated, it is also clear that mere acceptance of induction does not involve the inductee in any violations of the Nuremberg
principles. The principles of individual responsibility established at
Nuremberg would surely not regard the acceptance of induction as
itself a culpable act.

11. Insufficient attention is, I think, all too often given both to the different
kinds of cases that can arise and to the fact that principles appropriate to one
may not be appropriate (or as appropriate) to others. Any complete discussion
of the problems of individual responsibility in time of war would have to deal
with at least the following five kinds of cases and the similarities and differences
among them: (1) the combatant—the soldier on or near the battlefield; (2) the
draftee—the person who is subject to the selective service laws and who is
ordered, pursuant to those laws, to report for induction into the armed forces;
(3) the war supplier—the corporate executive who, on behalf of his corporation,
enters into a contract with the government to produce bullets or (perhaps a different case) napalm; (4) the senior advisor—the person, say Henry Kissinger or
W. W. Rostow, who enters government at a high level of decision-making and is
actively involved in the formulation and execution of the policies of war; (5) the
war resister—the person who violates the law in some serious way, including perhaps using violence against persons or things, with a view to thwarting, directly
or indirectly, the conduct of the war.

Other cases can obviously be imagined, and further distinctions among these
cases noted and discussed. The point I wish to emphasize is that these cases are
distinguishable and there are important differences among them that deserve not
to be obliterated.

12. Once again, any complete account of the complexities involved would distinguish the different forms that refusal (and perhaps even acceptance) might
take. That is to say, the person who is unwilling to accept induction can refuse
and (1) go to jail; (2) go underground; (3) flee to Canada; or (4) seek to procure
an exemption from service on fraudulent or spurious grounds. For my purposes,
but not for all morally relevant purposes, I lump together all of these alternatives
to accepting induction and characterize the case as one of either accepting or
refusing induction.

"Finally, he may not even be sent to Vietnam. And if he is, the laws of the United States afford him more than adequate protection there. If, when he gets to Vietnam, he is ordered specifically to do anything that constitutes one of the crimes defined in Article Six of the Charter, he has a right—even a duty—to disobey that order. Hence, he can avoid any personal liability by refusing to commit any war crimes if he is ordered to do so, and the law will not only excuse him from obedience, it will punish him for obedience. There is, therefore, simply no justification for refusing induction. Any references to Nuremberg at the stage of induction are not mistaken, they are bizarre. Whatever applicability they may have in other places and at other times, they have no conceivable or credible relevance at the moment of induction!"

Is this a convincing argument—or, more accurately, set of arguments? The first point, that the inductee ought to accept induction because the law requires him to do so, depends upon what is obviously a relevant but not a decisive consideration. This is a large issue and one that merits independent consideration of a sort that it is not possible to give here.[13] Its connection with the topic of this inquiry—the relevance of Nuremberg—will be brought out shortly. For the moment it is, I think, sufficient to observe that the acceptance of induction is relevant in two quite different respects. In the first place it is relevant because, all other things being equal, the fact that something is illegal helps to make it wrong to do it. Or to put the point somewhat differently (although perhaps no more clearly), we do have a prima facie obligation to obey the law and it is therefore prima facie wrong to disobey the law. But this is, of course, not to say very much, only that all other things being equal, it is wrong to disobey the law. In many cases, it is both right and obligatory to disobey it. In the second place, the fact that it is illegal to refuse to accept induction is relevant because it does reduce the inductee's culpability for accepting induction. Without adopting any particular view of the exculpatory character of the existence of penalties for disobedience, it is clear that there are reasonably severe penalties for disobedience of this law and that as a result some lesser degree of culpability for obedience ought to attach.

As I have said, the fact that the law requires the person to accept

13. I have dealt with this issue in considerably more detail in another paper entitled "The Obligation to Obey the Law," 10 *U.C.L.A. Law Review* 780 (1963).

induction cannot be a decisive consideration. Even if there is an obligation to obey the law, that obligation is only prima facie, not absolute. As a result, it is entirely possible, if not likely, that refusing to accept induction is one of those cases where the obligation is overridden by competing considerations and obligations. Consequently, the inductee may be justified in refusing to accept induction.

More to the point, however, is the question of whether he would be excused completely from culpability under either version or interpretation of Article Eight of the Charter by virtue of the penalties that accompany refusing to accept induction. It is apparent that the straightforward language of Article Eight would not excuse him, for, as we have seen, the existence of superior orders or laws is ruled out as an excuse and permitted only as a mitigating circumstance. But what about Article Eight as interpreted by the Tribunal at Nuremberg? What did the Tribunal mean when it said that an actor would be excused if moral choice were not possible? Is this a case where "moral choice" was not possible, and therefore where the Tribunal would, apparently, read in a complete defense?

To answer these questions we must first try to figure out what the Tribunal meant. Two interpretations come to mind. The most likely one is this. The mere fact that an actor had been ordered to do something does not by itself excuse the actor from responsibility for his actions. This is as it should be because, at a minimum, we must know something about both the stipulated consequences of disobedience and the likely consequences of disobedience before we can decide whether someone who acts in obedience to orders should be excused for his obedience. This is what the talk about the existence of "moral choice" comes to. Suppose, for instance, that there is a general standing order that soldiers are to kill rather than hold captive all enemy prisoners. At the very least, we would not want to excuse completely a soldier who complied with that order and shot all his prisoners until we knew a good deal more about such things as the announced penalty for disobeying that order, the probable penalty for disobedience, the typical soldier's reasonable beliefs about the penalty, and this soldier's belief as to what the penalty was. If the announced, probable, and understood penalty for disobedience were summary execution, the case would be a very different one from that where the penalty was demotion in rank. Thus, one interpretation of "moral choice" would focus heavily on the degree of choice exercisable by the actor. Where the penalty for disobedience is very great, and believed to be such, then one rationale for permitting the defense is that of excuse: in such circumstances a person will naturally, and perhaps inevitably, act in such a way as to avoid the penalty. He does not, we might say, "really have any choice," and so he is for this reason to be exempted from punishment.

A slightly different way to make the same point would focus not so much upon the absence of choice as upon the poignancy of the dilemma in which the actor finds himself. It is not that he cannot help himself when he seeks to avoid the punishment; it is rather that human beings, when caught up in such circumstances, simply ought not to be blamed for opting to save their own lives at the cost of other lives. People are not to be blamed, in other words, for failing to behave heroically or with such altruism that they bring consequences of a severely detrimental character upon themselves.

In either case, as I have said, the defense of superior orders would be a defense provided the accused could show that the choice involved was an illusory or unduly difficult one.[14]

14. At the risk of appearing excessively to hedge on every issue of moment, I must again acknowledge the existence of difficult issues that I have failed adequately to confront. Not the least of these is the role played by indoctrination and conditioning in affecting the nature of the choices that a person makes. Soldiers, for instance, are almost without exception taught, I imagine, that all orders are to be obeyed without question or serious reflection. What is more, a good deal of basic military training is devoted to developing within the soldier habits of obedience, so that the response to an order becomes a reflexive one. In such circumstances obedience to orders may, in some situations, take place without the presence of real choice of any kind.

In addition, even if a two-hour lecture on the laws of warfare and the duty to disobey "manifestly" illegal orders is interpolated somewhere in basic training, it is, I suspect, unrealistic psychology and doubtful morality to suppose that such a lecture appropriately weakens or loosens the habit of automatic obedience.

It is also worth observing that significant indoctrination of a special kind takes place in the case of the ordinary citizen. It is typically part of the citizen's conceptual apparatus—and a part that is often more difficult to oppose than we frequently suppose—that disobedience to the law is simply wrong and therefore that one has no choice (morally speaking) but to obey the law. Such a view is certainly part of the conceptual apparatus of many persons in England and America. Where persons genuinely hold such beliefs the case is stronger that the defense of superior orders should be a complete defense. Be that as it may, our resister can conceive of the appropriateness of disobedience to the law, and this defense is therefore not open to him.

A quite different interpretation of the "moral choice" requirement would be that which insisted upon emphasizing the *moral* character of the choice. Here the point would be that the results of the choice must be morally acceptable ones. This would be a tougher test to meet. Suppose the actor would suffer seriously and immediately should he refuse to obey the order. Still, in this view, he would be held accountable for failing to disobey if obedience to the order would result in the commission of a morally unacceptable action. To put the issue in rather extreme form: a soldier threatened with summary execution should he refuse to machine-gun innocent women and children would be held liable, because to choose to save his own life rather than the lives of women and children is not to make a moral choice.

None of this, however, by itself provides a convincing excuse for accepting rather than refusing induction. Is our prospective inductee to be excused if he accepts induction because according to any of these interpretations of the Tribunal's modification of Article Eight he has no "moral choice"? The answer is surely no. To be sure, the threat of a jail sentence of five years is not to be taken lightly. Nonetheless, it does not lead us easily to the image of someone rendered incapable of disobedience in the face of such a threatened punishment. Nor, on the other hand, does it confront the actor with the sort of dilemma in which he cannot be expected to do the right thing by disobeying.

This is, though, surely as it should be. A person who obeys a law, where the penalty for disobedience is five years in jail, is, all other things being equal, less culpable than one who takes the same action where there is no penalty for failing to do so, e.g., a person not subject to induction who volunteers for duty in the armed forces. But similarly, it is just not plausible to argue that the threat of five years in jail so deprives a person of choice or makes his choice so hard that he ought to be excused from culpability for his actions, no matter what those actions may be.

This is just to point up the fact that we are inclined, I think, to move on to the final part of the argument as the part that deserves the most careful attention. If the draftee ought to accept induction it is not because the threat of imprisonment excuses obedience to the order to accept induction. Rather, it is the lack of connection between accepting induction and thereby doing anything wrong that seems to be the crucial thing. Joining the armed forces, and especially through conscription, is, so the argument for the irrelevancy of Nuremberg goes, simply not the sort of action that is or was intended to be prohibited or punished in any way by either the Nuremberg Charter or Tribunal. Thus, any talk about Nuremberg as relevant to a refusal to accept induction is grossly misplaced. To accept induction into the armed forces is by no stretch of the imagination thereby to come within the principles of responsibility established at Nuremberg, regardless of what the United States may be doing in the way of violating the substantive provisions of Article Six of the Charter.

It should be evident from what has already been said that the issue is by no means as clear-cut as this argument would have it. A good deal will depend upon what we take Nuremberg to mean. The short answer is that the Charter can most reasonably be read to impose liability on the conscript; and even the modifications wrought by the judgment of the Tribunal do not very reasonably preclude this.

There are, it will be recalled, at least three potential sources of liability in the Charter. The first two can be considered together. One is the definition of crimes against peace as including the *waging* of aggressive war. What constitutes "waging" war? Arguably, "waging" war means fighting war. One fights a war most easily by being in an army. Hence anyone who is in an army that is engaged in a war of aggression is guilty of a crime against peace, to wit, waging aggressive war.

The second source is the doctrine of conspiracy and conspiratorial responsibility laid down in Article Six. That language, it may be recalled, proclaimed that: "Leaders, organizers, instigators and accomplices participating in the formulation or execution of a common plan or conspiracy to commit any of the foregoing crimes are responsible for all acts performed by any persons in execution of such plan."

Well, it is not hard to see the case for refusing induction. If the draftee accepts induction into the army he will, arguably, be deemed an accomplice who is by his service participating in the execution of a conspiracy to commit the crimes against peace, war crimes, and crimes against humanity that the United States is committing in Vietnam. And if this is the case, then the principle of vicarious liability laid down in the final portion of this section surely does inculpate him. As an accomplice participating in the conspiracy he is, under this principle, "responsible for all acts performed by any persons in execution of such plan." Thus, even if he remains safely at a base in the United States and never goes to Vietnam, he is chargeable with all of the crimes committed by the armed forces in Vietnam.

Now, what is there that would probably be said in reply? The Tribunal never did talk about what constituted "waging" war, so its interpretation of the Charter does not help. And while it did discuss the meaning and range of the conspiracy doctrine, this discussion is hardly decisive either. For in addition to limiting the conspiracy doctrine to conspiracies to commit crimes against peace (which will hardly relieve the anxiety of a conscript being drafted into an army that is waging a war of aggression), about all the Tribunal explicitly did was to announce that a person's actions must not be "too far removed from the time of decision and action" if conspiratorial liability is to attach, and the nature of the conspiracy must, in addition, be "clearly outlined in its criminal purpose."[15]

Indeed, the strongest argument available to those who reject the relevance of Nuremberg to our conscript is, theoretically, a rather queer argument to invoke. The more straightforward version of it would be that "waging" and "accomplice" are not to be interpreted as including the acceptance of conscription and subsequent service in the armed forces. As in many other matters of interpretation, there is no easy way to settle the point. Nonetheless, the argument would continue, there are reasons for adopting a reading of these terms that is sufficiently restrictive as to exclude the conscript. There is first the meaning of the terms in the context at hand. "Waging" war, being an "accomplice" were made crimes in a document that was intended by the drafters to provide a basis for prosecuting those who were, so to speak, the initiators of various horrendous wrongs. There was simply no thought, in the minds of the draftsmen, when they used these admittedly sweeping terms, that ordinary conscripts into the German Army would be held liable for accepting induction.

Moreover, there is indirect evidence that the Tribunal accepted such a restrictive interpretation of the Charter. It had, as has been indi-

15. *Trial of the Major War Criminals*, I, 225.

cated, no occasion to define what was involved in waging war, but it did have some opportunity to interpret the scope of the conspiracy provision. For at Nuremberg the prosecution had argued that all of the Nazi leaders and associates had a common plan that was generally understood by everyone who had a government position of any significance at all. Thus, all such officials were guilty of criminal participation in this plan, just as were all other persons who, knowing the Nazi plan, determined to assist it in ways open to them.

The Tribunal did not, apparently, accept this argument, although its opinion on this matter is neither very lengthy nor very clear. A person's action must not, said the Tribunal, be "too far removed from the time of decision and action" if liability is to attach on this ground. The nature of the conspiracy must in addition be "clearly outlined in its criminal purpose." Thus, not all supporters of a political program are guilty, nor are all persons whose actions aid the illegal plan in some minor, relatively indirect and unperceived way.

Even if this generally unenlightening elucidation of the Charter does give us a narrower test of complicity to work with, it is anything but clear how it would affect the case of the typical conscript in the United States today. Arguably, information about the character of the United States' participation in Southeast Asia is available to persons in the United States in a form in which comparable information was not available to German conscripts. Thus, persons who accept conscription into the United States Army do so having had a good opportunity to perceive the nature of the conspiracy they are thereby aiding and abetting. Under such circumstances, most conscripts will be in possession of the relevant facts, and there is nothing objectionable about holding them responsible.

The theoretically less straightforward and more curious answer to the conscript does not focus upon the language of the Charter or of the opinion of the Tribunal. It directs attention instead to the more general issue of how the Allies dealt with the Germans after the surrender. The answer is simple enough, even if the implications are not. Ordinary soldiers, and certainly conscripts, were in fact—so the argument goes—never, never prosecuted or blamed simply for having served in the army. Given the thousands of prosecutions that were conducted under the principles of the Charter, the one thing that stands out most forcefully is the fact that no prosecutions were even initiated on the ground that the accused had, by serving in the army, engaged in the waging of aggressive war or participated in a conspiracy to do so. The authorities never dreamed of regarding service in the army as a culpable act.

It is not obvious what we are to make of this argument, for, as I have said, it depends upon difficult and controversial theoretical notions. It involves a working out of the manner and degree to which certain practices determine the meaning that is properly to be given to rules and principles. The case is made more complicated because the practices that are here alleged to be involved are practices of abstinence—the nonprosecution of ordinary soldiers. And the problem is made more difficult still by the uncertain institutional setting of the entire Nuremberg enterprise and by the legitimate doubts which all persons ought to have about the easy assimilation of those proceedings to the typical operation of the criminal law.

Fortunately, for the purpose of our present inquiry we do not have to resolve any of these issues. It is possible, I think, to see the outlines of what the case against the applicability of Nuremberg to the conscript would look like. The case is a coherent and intelligible one. It is by no means, though, a strongly convincing one. It is by no means the sort of case that exposes as pretense or farce the contrary position. Indeed, the stronger case is clearly on the other side. If a person were genuinely and sincerely concerned scrupulously to attempt to conform his conduct to the principles established in the Nuremberg Charter and applied by the Tribunal at Nuremberg, he could most appropriately conclude that the acceptance of conscription would bring him into conflict with those principles.

III

But even if this concern with the meaning of "waging" and "accomplice" leaves the skeptic unconvinced of the relevance of Nuremberg to the conscript, there is one additional argument that the conscript could invoke with appreciable plausibility. It goes like this. Even if we assume that accepting conscription does not make one liable under any of the Nuremberg principles, still, accepting conscription may place the draftee in a causal chain from which escape will sub-

sequently become less and less easy and where potential liability will
be more and more likely. For, the argument would go, disobedience
to orders—even illegal ones—will be much more difficult once one is
in the army than disobedience to the selective service laws is now.
And once one gets shipped to Vietnam the situation is more difficult
still. In part, it is more difficult because one will then be confronted
with situations in which one will be encouraged, if not ordered, to
commit violations of the laws of war. While it is true that one theoretically can fall back upon the absence of moral choice here, as well as
upon the protections given under United States law to a soldier who
disobeys an illegal command, it is also true that these protections are
more apparent than real. For in such circumstances one can have little
confidence in the ability to make and to have made the distinctions
upon which these defenses rest.

And there is a related point. Our conscript might know enough
about what combat will be like to distrust his own ability to behave
properly once he is thrust into the combat situation. War, he might
argue, is extremely corruptive, particularly of the ability to make and
abide by morally credible decisions. This is surely one of the lessons
of Mylai. Consequently, it is both prudent and proper to avoid getting put into a position where one will be unable to behave properly.
Indeed, one is culpable here for the same reason that a person who
commits a vehicular homicide while intoxicated is culpable for getting
himself into a state where he cannot drive a car carefully. Refusing
to accept induction is therefore the last clear chance, so to speak, that
the conscript has to avoid being placed in a situation in which it is
very likely that he will find himself either unwilling or unable, or both,
to restrain himself from committing the crimes enumerated in Article
Six of the Charter.

For those who are concerned always to be "tough-minded" and "realistic" in any discussions of war, this should prove a particularly difficult argument to refute. It is far more convincing than the counterargument, which talks so glibly about the soldier's right (or duty) even
in combat to disobey a manifestly illegal order, arrest his superior officer as a war criminal, etc. If it is "pragmatic" arguments that will move
people, pragmatism is all on the side of the conscript who opts out
now, before he is required, while in the midst of the jungle, to reject

the law of the jungle and in the most unlikely of situations apply the niceties of international law and convention.

IV

In the discussion so far I have presupposed that the Nuremberg principles are the obvious place to look if one wants to get clear about an individual's responsibilities in time of war. And, as I indicated at the beginning, Nuremberg is surely the most common focus of those who are involved in serious and substantial opposition to the war in Vietnam. I now want to examine that supposition more closely. In particular, I want to try to establish two points that are not made as often or as clearly as I think they should be. The first is that there are several quite distinct respects in which the Nuremberg principles might be relevant to questions of responsibility and obligation. It is important to see what these are and how they differ from each other. The second is that there is also a danger in concentrating upon Nuremberg. Preoccupation with Nuremberg may lead us to exalt faulty principles of responsibility. It can also obscure the more fundamental moral issues that are at stake in a determination of an individual's responsibilities in time of war. I will look first at the different ways in which Nuremberg might be relevant, and then at the way in which recourse to Nuremberg can distort the analysis.

The first and most obvious reason why someone would be interested in the Nuremberg principles is to assess his potential liability under them. That is to say, the principles purport to define and establish certain substantive crimes and certain principles of criminal liability. In the words of the Tribunal: "It is the very essence of the Charter that individuals have international duties which transcend the national obligations of obedience imposed by the individual state. . . . Crimes against international law are committed by men, not by abstract entities, and only by punishing individuals who commit such crimes can the provisions of international law be enforced."[16] A legitimate and central portion of anyone's concern with the criminal law is to learn what the prohibitions are, what the penalties are, and what the likelihood is of getting caught and being punished. At Nuremberg and at the large number of other war crimes trials, numerous persons were

16. *Ibid.*, p. 223.

tried for having committed various crimes and were punished by sentences that included in some cases execution. Hence, it might be assumed, everyone ought to be interested in getting straight about potential liability under the Nuremberg principles, just because the penalties for violation can be very severe, and wartime is the one clear case in which the principles are likely to be applicable.

I think it somewhat curious that although this is an obvious respect in which Nuremberg is relevant, it is not in practice an important respect. By this I mean that I do not think very many of the persons who seek to raise the issue of Nuremberg in respect to their actions do so because they are genuinely fearful that they may in fact be punished for committing a Nuremberg offense.

It is fairly easy to see why this is so. There is no international criminal court before which violators can be brought. It is unlikely that the United States will lose the war in Vietnam in the sense that, say, the Germans lost World War II. To be sure, our conscript may be concerned with the threat of punishment as a war criminal by the Vietcong or the North Vietnamese, should he be sent to Vietnam and captured. Still, it is on the whole implausible to claim that possible punishment by the other side as a criminal lies at or near the core of our concern with the Nuremberg principles.

But the issue of sanctions and punishment is more complicated than I have made it out to be. There is, first of all, a sense in which the Nuremberg principles are a part of the domestic law of the United States. Hence, our conscript could argue that while external sanctions are remote, internal sanctions are not. He is concerned about Nuremberg because he is worried about being punished by United States courts for violating the criminal laws of the United States, of which the Nuremberg principles are a part.

This, too, is a sound position in theory, but once again, not so in practice. If there is one thing the draftee can be confident of in our generally uncertain world, it is that he will not be punished by a United States court for having accepted induction into the armed forces. Admittedly, the case of the soldier in the field is a bit different. As the three or four threatened prosecutions by United States courts for the commission of war crimes indicate, a soldier does run some very slight risk of punishment if he commits a war crime—but only, as

the Mylai massacre indicates, if he really runs amok and if by chance his actions receive unusual publicity back in the United States. At a minimum, a soldier runs an enormously greater risk of punishment if he seeks to invoke Nuremberg as a defense against a refusal to carry out a command than he does if he openly and voluntarily commits a war crime. He runs virtually no risk whatsoever if he simply follows his orders, whatever they may be. And he can be absolutely confident that he will not be punished for accepting induction.

I think this is worth noting for two reasons. On the one hand, it shows us that those who raise the matter of Nuremberg probably do not do so because they are genuinely anxious to avoid the *sanctions* that attended the violations determined to have been committed by the Germans and the Japanese. I do not mean by this that those who seek to invoke Nuremberg are disingenuous; rather, I mean that they are raising these issues in a context other than the most obvious one, the one in which we might expect interest in the criminal law to manifest itself.

On the other hand, the fact that Nuremberg is not a worry of this sort does tell us something of importance about the weakness and limitations of the entire Nuremberg undertaking. What the American experience shows is the practical, if not the theoretical, incapacity of national institutions to view their own behavior with sufficient objectivity to apply principles of this kind in any serious way to themselves. The courts in the United States are psychologically, if not logically, unable to assess governmental behavior in respect to war with sufficient detachment so as to take seriously the notion that, for example, the United States is guilty of war crimes and crimes against peace and humanity in Vietnam. This is worth attending to because it does call into question the fairness of the war crimes trials conducted after World War II and, more importantly, because it shows at least one respect in which the Nuremberg principles do differ markedly from other portions of our criminal law.

If it is unlikely that a concern to avoid penal sanctions flowing from a violation of the Nuremberg principles has been a central concern of those who have invoked Nuremberg in the course of their resistance to the war, what may be their interest in doing so? Several different points might be involved. To begin with, it is important to see that

Nuremberg can be relevant legally even though there is no chance of the courts of the United States being used as the institutions in which the genuine United States offenders against Nuremberg will be prosecuted. This other legal use arises because Nuremberg has a defensive as well as an offensive legal relevance. And, to the extent that Nuremberg has been invoked in the United States in a distinctively legal context, it has been in a defensive manner.

What do I mean by this? The Nuremberg principles were used offensively at Nuremberg. "Offensively" in the sense that they were used to impose criminal liability upon persons who were alleged to have violated the rules. They were used to *justify* the imposition of criminal responsibility. In the United States, with the exception of occasions like Mylai, the principles have been introduced defensively. "Defensively" in the sense that they have been invoked as a legal reason why a person ought not be held liable for violating the laws of the United States. They have been used to justify behavior which is ostensibly illegal but which, in the light of Nuremberg, is not. Thus, when Captain Levy refused to train Green Berets in medical skills and was subsequently court-martialed for his refusal, one of his defenses was that the Green Berets were committing war crimes in Vietnam. Hence, the illegality of their behavior justified him in refusing to assist them in developing their capabilities for action.

Similarly, when a conscript invokes Nuremberg in support of his refusal to accept induction, he is employing it defensively. He is arguing to the court that his apparently illegal act is really legal because of the legal superiority that the Nuremberg principles bear to the ordinary criminal laws of the United States.

There is nothing whatsoever wrong with this argument. Legally it is, I think, quite impeccable. Were I defending a resisting conscript in court, I would certainly urge the argument upon the court. I would do so, however, being most confident that the court would not really have anything to do with it. Not because it is bad legal theory, but because, as I have indicated, our courts (and probably the courts of any country) are unable to assume this degree of detachment from the society of which they are a part. This inability to be objective is but one of a number of like disabilities that judicial institutions—despite their claims of fairness and impartiality—labor under.

Almost certainly, this view is shared by those who do seek to interpose Nuremberg as a defense in our criminal courts. It is also, I suspect, the view of those who quite frequently appeal to the relevance of Nuremberg in a variety of nonlegal contexts. Hence a puzzle of sorts still remains. If people are not seriously worried about being punished as war criminals, and if they are convinced that the courts will not even recognize the force of a Nuremberg defense, why then all of the interest in and recourse to Nuremberg?

Part of the answer may be that people are, quite appropriately, concerned with the lawfulness of their behavior even when they are not concerned with avoiding the sanctions that accompany illegal behavior. To be able to claim that one is behaving in a fashion that the law permits (or even better, in a fashion that the law requires) is thereby to say something relevant about the rightness of one's conduct. Of course, it is not to say all that there is to say on the subject. But the fact that matters of legality and illegality are not morally *decisive* should not obscure for us their moral importance.

In addition, the nature of the criminal law is of special significance to us even when we are unconcerned with the question of sanctions. We are and ought to be concerned with the criminal law because it, more than the rest of the law, is a reasonably good guide to what constitutes seriously immoral behavior, Hence, people may be interested in the Nuremberg principles because, as criminal law, they are instructions as to how we ought to behave in time of war.

Still again, some persons may think the principles appropriate and important because they regard them as reasonable principles of behavior and liability in their own right—wholly apart from the fact that they are, in some sense or senses, the legally relevant principles. They appeal to Nuremberg, in other words, because they believe the Nuremberg principles to be the just principles of responsibility in respect to war.

Finally, over and above all of this, a number of persons sense, I suspect, that a special principle of justice is also at stake. They perceive, quite rightly, that the dominant accusatorial presence at and behind Nuremberg was the United States. They see it therefore as especially fitting that—irrespective of the intrinsic merit of the princi-

ples—the principles should govern the formulators of the principles
with at least the force with which the formulators insisted they should
apply to other malefactors.

All of these seem to me to be understandable, reasonable, and mod-
erately convincing arguments for insisting upon the relevance of
Nuremberg to individuals living today in the United States. But there
are dangers that accompany this insistence, and it is important that
these be understood as well. In particular, a preoccupation with
Nuremberg can serve—and to some degree, I think, has served—to distort much of the character of the fundamental opposition to the war.

The first danger is that it has appeared to rest opposition to the war
on the morally least interesting ground. Dependence upon Nuremberg
implies that if the behavior in question were not punishable, the actor
would not be behaving as he is. Despite the fact that persons who
appeal to Nuremberg are not really worried about the imposition of
sanctions if they go ahead and obey the laws of the United States
(say, by accepting induction), this is a very natural inference which
is to be drawn from any such invocation of Nuremberg. It is to suggest that a person is (for instance) resisting induction primarily, if
not solely, to avoid the imposition of the more severe sanction that
would attend accepting induction. It even suggests, although less
directly, that such a person would accept induction if only it weren't
prohibited by Nuremberg. And this, I think, obscures rather than illu-
minates both the reasons why most resisters do resist and why they
ought, on moral grounds, to resist. It substitutes a morally uninterest-
ing reason for acting—a kind of prudential concern with sanctions—
for a morally compelling reason for acting—a desire to prevent the
United States from continuing its horrendous behavior, and a desire
to avoid becoming morally implicated in the perpetration of grossly
immoral acts.

The second danger is the implication that the Nuremberg principles are obviously justifiable principles of substantive law and individual responsibility in respect to war. And this seems to me surely
wrong. At a minimum, the notions of conspiracy, conspiratorial liability, and group criminality all require a good deal more critical attention before we hail them as desirable components of any code of

criminal liability. Similarly, the rejection of the defense of superior orders (even as modified by the Tribunal) demands more thought than it has so far received.

The third and final danger is that which flows from the degree to which Nuremberg makes the issues legal issues. The point is partly that the criminal law is only a very rough guide to what is morally impermissible. Our own criminal laws punish persons and punish them severely for many things that they ought to be permitted to do. And these same laws permit persons to do things which no one ought to be permitted to do. So, the fact that behavior of a certain kind is illegal is neither a necessary nor sufficient assurance that it is wrong.

The more basic point, though, is that the fact that something is illegal is only one relevant consideration in the determination of its immorality. If a given course of conduct is illegal, we do know something about its immorality, but we surely do not know all there is to know. In the last analysis, the responsibilities that matter are an individual's moral responsibilities. Our legal responsibilities affect but by no means determine what those moral responsibilities are. A preoccupation with Nuremberg, with our legal responsibilities, can tend to deflect attention from what is surely the central concern: that individuals, especially in time of war, try to do the morally right and obligatory things.

DAVID MALAMENT

Selective Conscientious Objection and the *Gillette* Decision

The Military Selective Service Act provides for the deferment, on condition of alternate civilian service, of those "who, by reason of religious training and belief, [are] conscientiously opposed to participation in war in any form." In recent years considerable effort has been devoted to the interpretation of this clause, and in particular to the question of whether objectors to a particular war, so-called selective conscientious objectors, may qualify for exemption.

Many draft-age opponents of the Vietnam War have tried to convince their Selective Service Boards that, though not (necessarily) opposed to all wars, they are conscientiously opposed to the war the United States is now fighting. They and their lawyers have argued that (a) they are entitled to deferment under the existing provision *properly interpreted*; or (b) the Selective Service Act is unconstitutional to the extent that it discriminates against them. In 1968 a federal judge accepted the second claim and dismissed an indictment against a registrant who refused induction into the armed forces.[1] Several other favorable decisions followed.[2] But for the most part, the courts did not consider the claims of selective conscientious objectors favorably. The matter was decided by the Supreme Court last year in the case of *United States* v. *Gillette*. The Court upheld the denial of deferment to Gillette and his subsequent conviction "not because of doubt about the sincerity or religious character of his objection to

1. United States v. Sisson, 297 F. Supp. 902 (D. Mass. 1968).
2. United States v. Bowen, 2 SSLR 3421 (N.D. Calif. Dec. 24, 1969); and United States v. McFadden, 309 F. Supp. 502 (N.D. Calif. 1970).

military service, but because [his] objection ran to a particular war."[3]

The *Gillette* decision is questionable on several grounds. I hope to show this. But I am not primarily interested in the question of the constitutionality of the Selective Service Act. My layman's reply to the decision is rather a vehicle for the discussion of various claims about the difference between universal and selective conscientious objection and about why one, but not the other, should be grounds for deferment.

I

As a first line of defense, selective objectors have claimed that they qualify for deferment under the existing statutory provision, properly interpreted. The statute speaks of those who are "opposed to participation in war in any form." A first argument exploits the grammatical ambiguity in this clause. "In any form" seems to modify "war." If so, only universal objectors, that is pacifists, are eligible. But "in any form" may modify "participation." In this case the criterion of applicability is that the objector must oppose any form of participation in war. Such objection may then be interpreted plausibly as objection to any form of participation in some particular war, such as the war being waged at the time of conscription. This argument was accepted by at least one circuit court in a case dealing with a Jehovah's Witness. In fact, the court thought it *obvious* that "in any form" modified "participation."[4]

According to another interpretation of the disputed clause, "in any form" should be read as "in at least one form."[5] Hence the requirement is objection to participation in some war or other, presumably the one in which the objector would serve if drafted.

3. United States v. Gillette, 401 U.S. 437 (1971).

4. Taffs v. United States, 208 F.2d 331 (8th Circuit 1953). The relevant portion of the decision reads: "we are inclined to think that Congress did not intend such an unreasonable construction to be placed on this phrase. . . . The words, 'in any form' *obviously* relate, not to 'war' but to 'participation' in war. War, generally speaking, has only one form, a clash of opposing forces. But a person's participation therein may be in a variety of forms" (italics mine).

5. See Brief for Defendant, p. 21, United States v. Kurki, Crim. No. 65-CR-135 (E. Dist. Wisc.), cited in Ralph Potter, "Conscientious Objection to Particular Wars," *Religion and the Public Order*, ed. Donald A. Gianella (Ithaca, N.Y., 1968), p. 62.

Both these interpretations are, I think, farfetched. Justice Marshall, writing for the majority in *Gillette*, noted the possibility of alternate readings of the relevant clause but quickly dismissed it.[6] The debate in the Congress over the Selective Service Act suggests no reasonable doubt as to what was intended. It should be admitted that Congress had in mind both the common parse and the universal quantifier.

A second argument for qualification under the existing provision turns on the interpretation of "war." Many would-be conscientious objectors have told their draft boards that they would, under certain circumstances, "use force." The question obviously arises as to whether those circumstances constitute states of *war*. There are numerous judicial decisions to the effect that willingness to defend oneself, or a member of one's family, or a friend, or a stranger attacked on the street does not compromise the position of a conscientious objector. Nor do these decisions draw the line at defending groups of people or the immediate community in which one lives.[7]

On the basis of these precedents the argument is made that opposition to participation in war in any form is consistent with willingness to defend the country against attack. If the conscientious objector may legitimately defend his immediate community, then why not his entire town, or county, or state? Perhaps it is possible to defend oneself and one's family and neighbors only by banding with others and repelling invasion along national borders, rather than waiting for the invaders to reach Main Street.

A large class of would-be selective conscientious objectors would be protected if this argument were accepted. An opponent of the Vietnam War might take the position that while prepared to defend the country against attack, he would not fight in a war halfway around the world against a weak power with negligible air and naval capacity.

6. 401 U.S. at 443.

7. See, e.g., United States v. Purvis, 403 F.2d 563 (2d Circuit 1968), where it was held that: "Agreement that force can be used to restrain wrong doing especially as the last alternative, has little bearing on an attitude toward war. We would not expect a full-fledged conscientious objector to stand by while a madman sprayed Times Square with machine gun bullets, or while an assassin took aim at the President." See also United States v. Haughton, 413 F.2d 742 (9th Circuit 1969): "Haughton's willingness to use force to protect the community or to stop another from taking a life is consistent with conscientious objector status."

Whatever one thinks of the justice of the Vietnam War, it is surely wrong to think of it as a war of national defense against external attack.

Even if it were accepted, however, the argument would not be available to those would-be conscientious objectors who distinguish between just and unjust wars, declare their willingness to fight in behalf of a just cause, and also concede that there might be just wars which are not wars of national defense. Neither would it be available to Gillette, who in his request for classification as a conscientious objector stated his willingness to fight not only in a war of national defense but in a war sponsored by the United Nations as a peace-keeping measure as well. In the majority decision, the Supreme Court curtly dismissed this line of defense for Gillette. The language used suggests that the Court would not be impressed by the extrapolation from immediate and personal acts of defense to wars of national defense even if this were relevant to Gillette's case.[8]

Two further arguments have been advanced to the effect that certain types of selective objectors should qualify for deferment under the existing provision. One has to do with counterfactuals, the other with contingencies. Applicants for conscientious objector status are invariably asked by their boards whether they would have been willing to use force against Hitler in World War II, or whether they would use force under certain hypothetical conditions. Presumably an unequivocal negative answer is required of an applicant if he is to receive a deferment. Otherwise the applicant is merely a selective objector. But the argument can be made that unwillingness to answer these questions in the negative should not be grounds for disqualification.

An applicant might well reply to these questions by saying simply that he does not know what he would do. This answer, far from being evasive, might reflect the critical uncertainty of an honest man unwilling to make facile declarations about what he would do under extraordinary counterfactual conditions. This would-be conscientious objector feels certain that the particular war he faces is senseless, cruel, and immoral. He is quite sure that his conscience would give

8. 401 U.S. at 448.

him no peace were he to participate. He is furthermore drawn to the belief that all wars are futile and wrong, just as this particular one is. But he cannot dispel residual doubt about how he would react in the face of the excruciating circumstances that his draft board describes.

This hypothetical self-critical applicant recognizes that his principled rejection of war has never been put to a severe test. He recognizes that in the case of a genuine invasion his pacifist sympathies would come into conflict with strong impulses to defend other people. He cannot be sure how the conflict would resolve itself. In despair he might reach the conclusion that the alternative to war would be even worse than war itself.

These possibilities would plague the applicant faced with the question "what would he do if." Because of his personal integrity he would have to answer that he did not know. Some have argued that he should be considered a conscientious objector nonetheless. *As of the time of his application* he *is* opposed to participation in war in any form. That is the proper test, according to this argument, not what his position would be if the times were different.

There is something by way of precedent for this line of defense. In one case a registrant was asked by his board whether he would "change his mind" if the country were attacked. The registrant replied that it was *possible* that he would. On this basis the board denied his application for classification as a conscientious objector. But the district court ruled in his favor, saying that his reply should not disqualify him, "as it clearly relates to a contingency and provides no inference as to [his] state of mind when the incident occurred."[9]

This defense was dismissed as irrelevant in the *Gillette* decision. Thurgood Marshall saw an obvious difference between a universal objector who cannot exclude the possibility of a subsequent change of mind and an objector such as Gillette, who at time of application can name circumstances under which he would fight.[10]

A final argument for qualification of certain selective conscientious objectors under existing law concerns what might be called "contin-

9. United States v. Owen, 415 F.2d 390 (8th Circuit 1969). See also Miller v. Laird, 3 SSLR 3146 (N.D. Calif. April 28, 1970).
10. 401 U.S. at 448.

gent pacifism." A selective service registrant might well distinguish in principle between just and unjust wars, declare his willingness to fight in the former, and yet firmly believe that no actual war such as he might face would be just. This position might originate in a radical critique of American foreign policy. It might be based on the judgment that no war is just when waged with indiscriminate aerial weapons. Or it might derive from a theological doctrine which maintained that only a war ordained by God would be just and that God will (probably) not ordain such a war. This third possibility seems contrived, but it is in fact the example considered and considered favorably by several courts. It is more or less the position taken by Jehovah's Witnesses. Judges have wanted to consider them as conscientious objectors. There has never been any question of the sincerity of their rejection of secular war, or of their willingness to accept jail rather than conscription. But they will not declare opposition to participation in war in any form.

In 1955 the Supreme Court upheld the right of exemption of a Jehovah's Witness despite his declared willingness to participate "in defense of his ministry, Kingdom interests, and in defense of his fellow brethren."[11] Justifying the exemption, the Court noted that Jehovah had not commanded war of his Witnesses since Biblical times. But the Court did not seem to accept the implications of the decision. It later refused to hear a case involving a Roman Catholic who professed belief in the just war doctrine yet maintained that "there had never been a just war in history and there never could be."[12] Here denial of deferment and subsequent conviction for refusing induction were permitted to stand.

This line of defense, that an objector to a particular war is really a universal objector, contingently, is not directly relevant to *Gillette*. It is, however, interesting in its own right. The position is by no means contrived, and large numbers of objectors to the Vietnam War could in all honesty embrace it. At the same time the defense was not explicitly rejected by the Court in *Gillette*.

11. Sicurella v. United States, 348 U.S. 385 (1955).
12. United States v. Spiro, 384 F.2d 159 (3d Circuit 1967), *cert. denied*, 390 U.S. 956 (1968).

II

These four arguments may suggest how attorneys earn their fees but skirt the crucial question. What of the objector to a particular war such as the one in Vietnam who distinguishes that war from others that are just, who can say that he would fight in just wars, and who furthermore admits the possibility of such a war occurring within his lifetime? I think it must be conceded that it was not the intention of Congress to exempt such an objector. The question, then, is whether the draft law is unconstitutional insofar as it denies consideration to those "who, by reason of religious training and belief, [are] conscientiously opposed to participation" in the particular war they face. This is the question in *Gillette*.

The constitutional challenge is framed in two different ways. According to the first, forcing a man to fight in violation of religious conscience denies him his basic right to the "free exercise of religion" as guaranteed in the First Amendment. It is no less unconstitutional to deny this right to selective objectors than to universal objectors. Numerous religions forbid participation in particular wars without teaching pacifism. One thinks immediately of Catholic followers of the just war teachings of Augustine, Aquinas, Victoria, Suarez, and others.[13] Also, the United Church of Christ, the United Presbyterian Church, the American Baptist Church, and the World Council of Churches have passed resolutions recognizing the right of conscientious objection to particular wars.

In one recent case involving a Catholic, *United States* v. *McFadden*, a district court judge accepted the claim that the free exercise clause protected the defendant against prosecution for refusing induction.[14] The judge acknowledged that the government may abridge free exercise in the interests of "society's health and morals" by *proscribing* acts required by religious faith. But he distinguished these cases from those in which the state *coerces* action in violation of religious con-

---

13. For example, the Dominican Francisco Victoria, who helped formulate canon law in the sixteenth century, wrote: "If a subject is convinced of the injustice of a war, he ought not to serve in it, even on the command of his prince. This is clear, for no one can authorize the killing of an innocent person" (401 U.S. at 471 [Justice Douglas' dissent]).

14. 309 F. Supp. at 505, 506.

science. He further acknowledged that the killing of another human being without just cause, i.e., murder, is probably the most extreme violation of conscience that the government could coerce.

The government has consistently taken the position in response that exemption from military service on grounds of religious scruples is not a right protected by the free exercise clause or any other part of the Constitution.[15] Rather, exemption is a matter of "legislative grace," extended in particular circumstances for particular reasons. In *Gillette* and elsewhere the government argued that even the exemption available to Quakers is not absolute and that the Congress might withdraw it without violating the Constitution.

According to the second challenge, even if exemption for conscientious objectors is a matter of grace rather than right, the Selective Service Act is still unconstitutional because it creates invidious distinctions, rendering grace to some while denying it to others. Even if Quakers need not be exempted, in fact they are. And since they are, other sorts of religious objection to participation in war must receive the same protection they do. This challenge is framed in terms of the First Amendment stipulation that "Congress shall make no law respecting an establishment of religion," or under the "equal protection" clause. In another recent case, *United States* v. *Bowen*, an indictment against a Catholic draft refuser was dismissed on these grounds.[16]

The majority in *Gillette* rejected these challenges, but it made concessions along the way. The Court acknowledged that even if there is no absolute right to conscientious objector exemption, there are good reasons why the Congress might provide it. The Court recognized a public interest in protecting the individual conscience wherever possible. It conceded that "fundamental principles of conscience and

15. It has been argued that there is a "right not to kill" to be found in the Ninth Amendment, which states: "The enumeration in the Constitution of certain rights shall not be construed to deny or disparage others retained by the people." See Norman Redlich and Kenneth R. Feinberg, "Individual Conscience and Selective Conscientious Objection: The Right Not to Kill," 44 *New York University Law Review* 875-900 (Nov. 1969).

16. 2 SSLR at 3422, where Judge Weigel said: "In denying conscientious objector status to Bowen based upon his religious opposition to the Vietnam War but permitting it to one whose religious opposition is to all wars, the effect of Section 6j is to breach the neutrality between religion and religion as required by the mandate of the 1st Amendment."

religious duty may sometimes override the demands of the secular state." It acknowledged that there are relevant pragmatic considerations as well, such as "the hopelessness of converting a sincere conscientious objector into an effective fighting man."[17] It even conceded that these reasons for legislative grace apply to objection to particular wars just as much as they do to universal objection. The Court insisted, however, that the interest in protecting the free exercise of religious conscience is not absolute and must be balanced against competing constitutional interests, namely "providing for the common defense" and insuring that the burdens of defense are distributed equitably.

In response to the second challenge, the Court ruled that the line drawn between selective and universal objection does not establish or favor one religion over another. Clearly any number of laws may exercise an incidental discrimination among religions without doing so unconstitutionally. Criminal codes favor garden-variety religions over other, more zealous creeds which would wreak vengeance upon unrepentant sinners. But they do so for good secular reasons having nothing to do with an intent to found or foster or establish a religion. The line drawn between different sorts of religious objection to participation in war is justified similarly. We are told that "there are neutral secular reasons to justify the line," and as a result "it is neither arbitrary nor invidious."[18] These reasons, again, have to do with the national defense and the need to provide for it equitably. Both governmental interests are sufficiently weighty to justify any incidental discrimination between religious beliefs that the Act may require.

The Court's position is that provision for exemption of conscientious objectors must be evaluated in the light of conflicting legitimate interests, and that this is a proper matter for legislative determination. The Congress, presumably, had found that this balance of interests warranted exemption of only the universal objectors. It would have been neither "irrational" nor "unreasonable" for the Congress to have extended exemption to selective objectors.[19] But in acting as it did the Congress did not violate the Constitution.

In the *Sisson* case, the first important case won by a selective conscientious objector, Judge Wyzanski also found that "this is not an

17. 401 U.S. at 445, 453.   18. *Id.* at 449.   19. *Id.* at 460.

area of constitutional absolutism." He insisted that any and all men might be justly conscripted "in the last extremity." He held, however, that when Sisson refused induction we were nowhere near the last extremity, and that the public interest in conscripting Sisson *then* was clearly outweighed by the public interest in protecting the freedom of religious conscience.[20] In other words, the balance arrived at by the Congress was sufficiently lopsided to justify judicial intervention.

At least for the purposes of this essay, that is the position I take as well. According to the *Gillette* decision, Congress reasonably assumed that serious governmental interests would be jeopardized if conscientious objection privileges were extended to selective objectors. I shall argue that it is not at all clear that this would be the case. The government makes several different claims to this effect, but all are questionable.

III

Two governmental interests are mentioned in the decision. The first is that of fair administrability. The government warned that a program excusing selective objectors would be "impossible to conduct with any hope of reaching fair and consistent results." It would "involve a real danger of erratic and even discriminatory decision-making in administrative practice." The second interest is that of maintaining the effectiveness and morale of our armed forces.[21]

The test for eligibility as a conscientious objector which Gillette challenged consists of three parts: objection must be conscientious; it must be based on "religious training and belief"; and it must apply

20. 297 F. Supp. at 908. Judge Wyzanski stated: "The sincerely conscientious man, whose principles flow from reflection, education, practice, sensitivity to competing claims, and a search for a meaningful life, always brings impressive credentials. When he honestly believes that he will act wrongly if he kills, his claim obviously has great magnitude. That magnitude is not appreciably lessened if his belief relates not to war in general but to a particular war or a particular type of war. . . . It is equally plain that when a nation is fighting for its very existence there are public and private interests of great magnitude in conscripting for the common defense all available resources, including manpower for combat. *But a campaign fought with limited forces for limited objects with no likelihood of a battlefront within this country and without a declaration of war is not a claim of comparable magnitude*" (italics mine).

21. 401 U.S. at 456, 455.

to participation in war in any form. The government's central claim, accepted by the Court, was that if the third part of the test were dropped, it would be essentially more difficult to administer fairly and consistently than it is as it now stands. In Thurgood Marshall's words:

> A virtually limitless variety of beliefs are subsumable under the rubric, "objection to a particular war." All the factors that might go into nonconscientious dissent from policy, also might appear as the concrete basis of an objection that has roots in conscience and religion. Indeed, *over the realm of possible situations, opposition to a particular war may more likely be political and nonconscientious than otherwise. The difficulties of sorting out the two, with a sure hand, are considerable.* . . . In short, it is not at all obvious in theory what sorts of objections should be deemed sufficient to excuse an objector, and there is considerable force in the Government's contention that a program of excusing objectors to particular wars may be "impossible to conduct with any hope of reaching fair and consistent results. . . ."[22]

The Court is concerned about the administrative difficulty of answering two questions: first, whether an objection is conscientious, and second, whether the objection is religious in the proper sense, rather than political. The Court seems to accept the claim that these determinations would not be merely more difficult to make in the case of selective objection, but so much more difficult that fair administration of the Selective Service Act would be impossible. In order to evaluate this claim, which is central to the Court's decision, it is necessary to review how the Court has previously interpreted the first two parts of the three-part test for eligibility as a conscientious objector.

The first federal conscription bill that made provision for conscientious objectors was enacted during World War I. It provided exemption only to members of historic peace churches, such as Quakers and Mennonites. The next bill, in 1940, made no mention of membership in a traditionally recognized religious organization, but provided exemption for those "who, by reason of religious training and belief, [are] conscientiously opposed to participation in war in any form." In 1948 a qualifying sentence was added: "Religious training and

22. *Id.* at 455-456 (italics mine).

belief in this connection means an individual's belief in a relation to a Supreme Being involving duties superior to those arising from any human relation, but does not include essentially political, sociological, or philosophical views, or a merely personal moral code."

The qualification was added to clarify matters, but it had the opposite effect. In a series of cases the "Supreme Being" test was challenged as being prejudicially narrow, since it excluded such religions as "secular humanism." The distinction between religious beliefs and those stemming from a "personal moral code" was also challenged as being vague, arbitrary, or discriminatory.

The Supreme Court came to accept these challenges in the *Seeger* decision in 1965. In his application Seeger had refused either to affirm or deny belief in a Supreme Being. He had crossed out the words "training and" in the phrase "religious training and belief" and put quotation marks around "religious." The Court decided that he qualified as a conscientious objector nevertheless. It formulated what has become known as the "equivalency test" of religious belief. What is required is "a sincere and meaningful belief which occupies in the life of the possessor a place parallel to that filled by the God of those admittedly qualifying for exemption."[23]

In response to *Seeger* the Congress deleted the Supreme Being clause in 1967, but left the second half of the qualification, that religious training and belief "does not include essentially political, sociological, or philosophical views, or a merely personal moral code." The Selective Service Act was in that form when Gillette violated it and it has not been changed since.

In its decision in *Welsh* in 1970 the Court went further and interpreted away some of the force of the restrictive clause about merely personal moral codes. Welsh simply struck out the words "religious training and belief" when filling out his application and described himself as a humanist, much as Gillette did. The Court decided, nonetheless, that his position was religious in the proper sense and that he should not have been denied his classification. It applied the following test: "If an individual deeply and sincerely holds beliefs which are purely ethical or moral in source and content but which nevertheless impose upon him a duty of conscience to refrain from participat-

23. United States v. Seeger, 380 U.S. 176 (1965).

ing in any war at any time, he is entitled to deferment as a conscientious objector."[24] As of the time it heard Gillette's appeal, this was the Court's criterion for eligibility as a conscientious objector. It reaffirmed this position in the course of its decision in *Gillette*. Thus if the Court is to distinguish political from religious objection, and contend further that selective objection is "likely to be political," it is bound to interpret religion in this sense, which does not exclude secular conscience.

What is the distinction? The Court never gives an example, but I assume it would consider political the following reasons for opposing a particular war: (a) the war is one of imperialist intervention; (b) it is contrary to the interests of the international working class; or (c) it is contrary to the national interest (of the country in whose army the objector is asked to fight). I further assume that it would have to consider an objection based on the Christian just war doctrine to be properly religious. According to one formulation, the doctrine forbids participation in a war when any of the following conditions are not met: "(1) The cause must be just. (2) War must be the last resort, the only possible means of securing justice. (3) War must be made by lawful public authority. (4) There must be a reasonable hope of victory. (5) The intention of the government declaring war must be just, that is, free of vindictive hatred, greed, cruelty, or glee. (6) There must be a due proportion between the good probably to be accomplished and the probable evil effects of the war. (7) The war must be rightly conducted through the use only of just means."[25] The question is how these conditions, or rather their respective negations, are different from (a), (b), and (c).

I do not question that objections such as (a), (b), or (c) are in a good sense political in character. So are all normative judgments about the affairs of a national state, polis, or other body politic. The Christian doctrine that defines the conditions under which war is justified is itself political. But the sense in which these judgments are political is not incompatible with derivation from "religious training and belief" as the phrase is interpreted in *Seeger* and *Welsh*, or even

24. United States v. Welsh, 398 U.S. 340 (1970).
25. Potter, "Conscientious Objection to Particular Wars," *Religion and the Public Order*, p. 68.

in the most traditional interpretation. God might reveal his will concerning the affairs of state and command men to act accordingly. He often did so in Biblical times. Jehovah's Witnesses are still waiting for Him to do so again.

A draft-age registrant might oppose a war on grounds (a), (b), or (c) precisely because of his "religious training and belief." An observant Catholic might refuse to participate in what he considered to be a war of imperialist intervention because he also thought such wars violated at least several of the conditions defining a just war. Another citizen who believed his country to be of divine importance might refuse to participate in a given war if he felt the war threatened the interests of the country.

It should also be clear that normative principles concerning warfare which we traditionally associate with religious sects can be shared by nonbelievers. The Christian just war doctrine, which the Court must recognize as a possible religious foundation for selective objection, is not at all sectarian.[26] Quite the contrary. Some of the principles of the doctrine have even been incorporated into the body of international law which defines the permissible circumstances and means of war. One might embrace the just war doctrine as the will of God as revealed in personal mystical communion or through the mediation of a long heritage of religious teachings. But one might also embrace its criteria within a different framework: as a secular moral intuitionist, as a contractarian,[27] or as a utilitarian of one sort or another. And one might do so with such depth of conviction as to satisfy the Court's "equivalency test" that belief be religious.

Of course not every objection to war couched in political language need reflect deeply felt moral obligations or the dictates of conscience.

---

26. According to John Courtney Murray, S.J., who served on the National Commission on Selective Service (in dissent), "it is not a sectarian doctrine. It is not exclusively Roman Catholic; in certain forms of its presentation, it is not even Christian. It emerges in the minds of all men of reason and good will when they face two inevitable questions. First, what are the norms that govern recourse to the violence of war? Second, what are the norms that govern the measure of violence to be used in war? . . . The . . . doctrine . . . insists, first, that military decisions are a species of political decisions, and second, that political decisions must be viewed, not simply in the perspectives of politics as an exercise of power, but of morality and theology in some valid sense" ("War and Conscience," *A Conflict of Loyalties*, ed. James Finn [New York, 1968], p. 21).

27. See John Rawls, *A Theory of Justice* (Cambridge, Mass., 1971), sec. 58.

But neither is this necessarily the case with objection couched in what the Court would probably consider religious language. In worrying about whether objection is political the Court is worrying about the wrong question.

The force of *Seeger* and *Welsh* was to collapse the condition that objection be based on religious training and belief into the condition that it be conscientious, i.e., that it be deeply and sincerely held and derive from the binding obligations of conscience, divinely inspired or not. The proper question for administrative determination is whether a draft-age opponent of a given war is conscientious in this sense.

The government's central claim, accepted by the Court, is that this determination is harder to make when objection is framed with respect to a particular war than when it is framed with respect to all wars. The determination, in fact, is so difficult that a program excusing selective objectors would be "impossible to conduct with any hope of reaching fair and consistent results." I cannot see why it would be harder to conduct than the present program. I certainly cannot see why it would be "impossible" to conduct. And yet surely only insuperable administrative difficulty, not mere administrative inconvenience, is the sort of governmental interest which may be weighed against basic rights as guaranteed in the free exercise, nonestablishment, and equal protection clauses of the Constitution.

Admittedly, in individual cases it may be difficult to determine whether a would-be conscientious objector is truly conscientious. But in these cases the difficulty has nothing to do with whether his objection is particular or universal. There is a confusion here between the substance of a position relating to the justifiability of war and the sincerity of an applicant who claims to embrace the position on grounds of conscience. The fact that a man *claims* opposition to all wars is no proof that he qualifies for deferment. It simply happens to be the case that people who have traditionally claimed opposition to all wars— Quakers, for example—have more than proven their conscientiousness in our eyes. We naturally tend to associate all objectors with them.

The Selective Service System does not accept claims to conscientious objection at face value. A personal statement, references, and an interview are required. The local draft boards have the responsibility for judging depth and sincerity of belief on the basis of this evidence. Decisions may be appealed and all determinations are subject to review in the federal courts. The mechanisms whereby we evaluate sincerity and intent are surely fallible and subjective, but they are not more so in the case of claims of selective objection than in those of universal objection. In fact a would-be selective objector, unlike his counterpart, may properly be held accountable for substantive information about the nature of the war he opposes. This might actually facilitate an evaluation of his conscientiousness. Furthermore, however imperfect our ability to judge states of mind, juries make such judgments every day in cases where intent or sincerity is a factor in the determination of guilt.

The Court elaborates upon the difficulty of processing would-be selective conscientious objectors by listing three specific worries. First, "an objector's claim to exemption might be based on some feature of a conflict which most would regard as incidental, or might be predicated on a view of the facts which most would regard as mistaken."[28] For instance, one might oppose the war in Vietnam *simply* because it threatened the extinction of rare flora in the Mekong Delta, or because Ho Chi Minh was a Sagittarius. These would indeed be difficult cases to administer. It would have to be determined whether the applicant was possessed of a deeply felt moral obligation to preserve rare flora or to act in accord with cosmic command. But such cases would not be more difficult to administer than one in which a registrant opposed *all* war out of concern for the natural flora, rather than for human beings, or because he himself was born under a pacific sign.

Furthermore, it should be recognized that very few objectors, if any, would base their objection "on some feature of a conflict which most would regard as incidental." The overwhelming majority of draft-age opponents of the Vietnam War base their opposition on the belief that, at the very least, it is causing death, injury, destruction, and human misery completely out of proportion to any good that might come of it. These "features" are not incidental.

Neither does it seem especially significant that objection to a particular war might be "predicated on a view of the facts which most would regard as mistaken." As long as objectors to the war are in the

28. 401 U.S. at 456, 457.

minority this will surely be the case. But the majority, of course, may be wrong about the facts. There was a time when the majority in this country accepted the government's claim that it was defending the sovereign state of South Vietnam against unprovoked attack from the North. Perhaps the majority still does. Further, even if we could say objectively that the majority view was correct, those who failed to recognize this might still be conscientious. Speaking to this very point, the Court held in *Seeger* that: "the 'truth' of a belief is not open to question"; rather, the question is whether the objector's beliefs are "truly held."[29]

Second, the Court notes that "the belief that a particular war at a particular time is unjust is by its nature changeable and subject to nullification by changing events."[30] Admittedly an objection to a particular war might change as the war evolved. For example, at the outbreak of World War II there were British socialist conscientious objectors who opposed the war because it pitted working men against one another. Some of them may have changed their minds after Germany invaded Russia in the summer of 1941. They may have then felt that the interests of the international working class, on balance, would best be advanced by Germany's defeat. But the fact that they did change their evaluation of the justness of the war does not necessarily compromise the initial conscientiousness of their objection. Had they meant simply to ride out their deferments they would not have aired their views publicly. They certainly would not have propagandized them.

Changeability of beliefs is a possible difficulty in the evaluation of claims to universal objection as well. A person might be opposed to participation in all wars because he has concluded after long historical research that in fact all wars cause more evil than good in the end. Yet during the course of the particular war he faces he might learn of new enemy atrocities more horrid than any he had ever imagined possible. As a result he might come to believe that this was an instance, a first instance, of a war which was just. Bertrand Russell, who considered himself more or less a pacifist during World War I

29. 380 U.S. at 185.   30. 401 U.S. at 456.

and at the outbreak of World War II, eventually came to support the latter.[31]

Though objectors to particular wars, even when conscientious, may change their positions, it does not follow that they should not be deferred. Rather it follows that conscientious objector classifications should be subject to periodic review in precisely the way certain medical, occupational, and hardship deferments are. The Selective Service System manages to review these claims regularly even though their number dwarfs that of conscientious objection claims.

Third, the Court acknowledges the government's claim that expansion of exemption provisions would discriminate in favor of the "articulate, better educated, or better counseled." The proper response to this is the same as to the first and second difficulties outlined by the Court. Whatever advantage a well-counseled college graduate might have before his board he will have whether he tries to convince it of the conscientiousness of his objection to one war or to all wars.

The government that here professes such concern for the inarticulate and poorly educated might better have occupied itself with suggesting improvements in the administrative procedure for evaluating conscientious objection claims. The tribunals that evaluate such claims should be separate from the draft boards, whose principal concern is one of filling monthly quotas and whose members are rarely known for their tolerance or judicial insight. England maintained a separate tribunal system until it ended conscription in 1960.

In summary, I do not see why it should be essentially more difficult to judge the conscientiousness of a selective objection to military service than it is to judge the conscientiousness of a universal objection. Concern for the possibility of fair administration might have been more appropriate when the Court by its interpretation liberalized the sense in which it is required that objection derive from "religious training and belief." If church affiliation were the test, as was formerly the case, then applications would be comparatively easy to process. But the Court was reluctant to construe religious conviction narrowly and thereby risk favoring one religion over another. For precisely

31. Bertrand Russell, *Autobiography: The Middle Years* (New York, 1968), p. 275.

this reason it should not now favor one sort of conscientious objection to war over another.

IV

The second substantial government interest mentioned by the Court in *Gillette* is that of maintaining the effectiveness and morale of our armed forces. If selective objectors were permitted to perform alternate civilian service or noncombatant military service, it is possible that there would not be enough men left to fill army quotas. Even if soldiers were available in sufficient numbers, some might resent the exemption of others, and this resentment would "weaken the resolve" required of fighting men.[32]

The first contention, that deferment of selective objectors would significantly deplete available manpower, is, of course, an embarrassing one for the government. Relative to the total numbers available for service, very few men have been drafted to fight in the Vietnam War. In considering the government interest in maintaining the effectiveness of the armed forces the Court refers to the Report of the National Advisory Commission on Selective Service, released in 1967. In April 1967, the month in which Gillette applied for conscientious objector status, Burke Marshall, Chairman of the Commission, testified that the problem before the Selective Service System was how to select 110,000 men out of the 730,000 available.[33] Actually the figure of 730,000 is misleading, since the selection process begins long before that figure is reached. In 1968, of 20,829,000 registrants aged 18½ to 26, some 2,200,000 had student deferments, 4,126,000 were deferred on the basis of fatherhood or hardship, 471,000 had

32. 401 U.S. at 459-460: "The fear of the National Advisory Commission on Selective Service, apparently, is that exemption of objectors to particular wars would weaken the resolve of those who otherwise would feel themselves bound to serve despite personal cost, uneasiness at the prospect of violence, or even serious moral reservations or policy objections concerning the particular conflict."

33. Hearings of the Senate Committee on Armed Services, 12-19 April 1967, cited in Brief for Defendant, p. 53, United States v. Sisson, *cert. denied,* 399 U.S. 267 (1970).

occupational or agricultural deferments, and some 424,000 were unclassified.[34]

If so many men were conscientiously opposed to a given war that it became impossible to fill even a small quota, then it would be questionable whether the government was justified in going to war in the first place, or in using conscripts to do so. In fact, however, much to the disappointment of war opponents, the number of men conscientiously opposed to service in recent years has never been large enough to threaten army quotas. Volunteers have always been in the majority; their proportion might have been still larger if the army had raised its salaries and benefits, as it has done more recently. Furthermore, many of the men who might have been selective conscientious objectors qualified simultaneously for student or occupational deferments.

It can be said in response that the government is concerned about manpower needs not only under present circumstances, but also in anticipation of future war on a larger scale. Deferment of selective objectors might set a bad precedent. I do not find this argument compelling either. For one thing, the nature of modern warfare is such that vast infantry forces may never be used again. "War on a larger scale" is likely to be conducted by remote control by highly trained technicians and experts, none of whom will be conscripts. Even now the army is moving toward an all-volunteer status, and the savage air war over Indochina is increasingly automated.

However, even if there were a future conflict in which the national defense required the conscription of large infantry forces, the government would not then be crippled by a precedent from the period of the Vietnam War, when conditions were essentially different. To rule that it is unconstitutional to withhold conscientious objector status from Gillette under present circumstances is not to deny that all men, including Gillette and Quakers, might be justly conscripted "in the last extremity."

Though conceding for purposes of argument that conscription of all available manpower might be justified under conditions of extreme emergency, of clear national danger, I should think that those conditions would make conscription unnecessary. The extent of the danger

34. *Statistical Abstract of the United States,* 90th edn. (Washington, D.C., 1969), p. 260, table 383 (cited in Sisson brief, p. 54).

would be clear to the vast majority of citizens and they would accept the burden of self-defense voluntarily. Indeed, a national plebiscite in the form of a call for volunteers is probably a better test of the extent to which war is necessary and justified than an executive order to raise draft calls and commit troops, or even a Congressional declaration of war. I am far more concerned about men agreeing to fight when they are not endangered simply because their government orders them to do so than about them refusing to fight when genuine need arises. This is an argument against conscription, but it is also an argument for the recognition of selective conscientious objectors. Under those rare conditions of national emergency when conscription is justified, few men will be conscientiously opposed to participation.

The experience of the British during World War II is significant in this context. Their provision for conscientious objection made no mention of religion, nor did it specify that objection must be to all war as against the one war at hand.[35] The National Service Act of 1939 provided that any person who claimed that: "he conscientiously objects (a) To be registered in the military service register, or (b) To performing military service, or (c) To performing combatant duties . . . may apply . . . to be registered as a conscientious objector." If found to qualify, objectors of the first sort would be unconditionally exempted; those of the second would be exempted from military service on condition of civilian service; those of the third would have to perform noncombatant military duty.

Up to the end of hostilities in August 1945, 67,000 men had provisionally registered (i.e., applied for recognition) as conscientious objectors. This figure represents about .8 percent of the total number registered. The percentage fell from 1.8 percent in the prewar registration to under .6 percent of all registrations after June 1940 and to under .5 percent of all registrations after February 1941. The British local and appellate tribunals that heard these cases found in favor of

35. Fenner Brockway (now Lord Brockway) describes it as follows: "The test was not the ground of objection but the depth of the objection. If an applicant convinced them that he held his convictions so rootedly that they represented to him an issue of right and wrong in his own conduct they exempted him, despite the fact that in another war he might take up arms" (in his preface to Denis Hayes, *Challenge to Conscience* [London, 1949], cited in Brief for Defendant, p. 76, United States v. Gillette, 401 U.S. 437).

approximately 80 percent of all those who applied.[36] By way of contrast, in June 1971 there were in this country 34,202 selective service registrants classified as conscientious objectors. They represented 1.11 percent of the total number registered, and between 40 to 60 percent of the number who had applied for the deferment. Hence between 1.9 to 2.8 percent of all registrants applied for classification as conscientious objectors despite the more stringent requirements.[37] Great Britain, at a time when it was seriously endangered, when there was even a possibility of invasion, managed to tolerate the conscience of selective objectors. The United States is not comparably endangered now, nor was it so even during World War II.

The British system did not work flawlessly. Particularly in the beginning, there were discrepancies between local tribunals, so that, for instance, some were more likely to be lenient toward socialist objectors than others.[38] But in time the policies became more uniform, at least as measured statistically. Even the outspoken, militant leadership of the conscientious objection movement acknowledged that the tribunals "with some exceptions, fulfilled their impossible task with sympathy and insight."[39]

The example of Great Britain is relevant not only to the government's concern about having available sufficient manpower for an army, but also to its claim that deferment of selective objectors might cause resentment and corrode morale among conscripts within the

36. The breakdown by type of classification was as follows:

Percentage of CO claims accepted	79.4
(a) unconditionally	6.1
(b) conditionally	48.5
(c) for noncombatant service	24.8
Percentage of claims rejected	20.6

All figures are from *Conscription: A World Survey*, ed. Devi Prasad and Tony Smythe (London, 1968), p. 59.

37. Figures released by the Selective Service System and reprinted in the *Reporter for Conscience Sake* (published by the National Interreligious Service Board for Conscientious Objectors) 28, no. 9 (Sept. 1971): 3.

38. See the *CO's Hansard* (London), a series of reprints from parliamentary reports of matters concerning the conscientious objector, published by the Central Board for Conscientious Objectors; e.g., Pamphlet no. 3 (April 1940), p. 10.

39. Fenner Brockway, *Objection Overruled*, the Ninth Annual Report of the Central Board for Conscientious Objectors (London, 1948), p. 6.

army. Britain's army managed well enough even though there probably was some resentment of "conchies."

Granted the problem is much more serious when a war is as unpopular as the present American war and has produced so great a national polarization. There are undoubtedly large numbers of conscripts who are not prepared to declare themselves as conscientious objectors but who nevertheless serve only because they feel it their duty. They may have reservations about the justice or necessity of the war, or may simply be concerned about the inconvenience or danger involved in military service—quite rightly so. This reluctant conscript might well think it unfair that his more zealous neighbor, even if conscientious, is permitted alternate service or noncombatant military service. Once such a conscript is ordered to Vietnam, or when he first sees combat, he might well be resentful.

This objection could be directed to the deferment of universal objectors as well as to selective objectors, but not with the same force. Pacifists, like celibates perhaps, are considered odd but usually tolerable. The selective objector, however, presents a more focused dissent and may arouse greater anger. There is a difference between telling a businessman that all business is corrupt and telling him that a particular business practice in which he is engaged is dishonest.[40]

A reluctant conscript may feel duty-bound to serve, but only if the onerous duty is shared fairly. His position is entirely justified. The question is whether *fairness* is compromised when the selective objector is permitted alternate service. Though he may not recognize it, even the reluctant conscript has an interest in the public tolerance of conscientious objection, selective or universal. Could he abstract himself from the given war and knowledge of his own response to it, he might well imagine being in the intolerable position of the conscientious objector himself. He might consider the awful choice of going to jail or fighting in conflict with conscience. As he would want to be protected in that situation, so he would recognize the need to protect others and to institutionalize a third possibility. True, some shirkers might slip through. But they would probably not be many, and their escape would be less important *to him* than the possibility of imprison-

40. The example is used in Brief for Defendant, p. 111, United States v. Sisson, 297 F. Supp. 902.

ment for himself—or his son. This, I think, might be the view of an objective representative citizen. To the extent that he would endorse deferment of selective objectors wherever possible, the practice is not unfair.

It might be argued, however, that idealized considerations of fairness are irrelevant. Even if army morale *should* not be influenced by the deferment of selective objectors, in fact it might be. The government's concern, the argument repeats, must be considered against the bitter background of the Vietnam War and not against idealized models of political justice.

This sort of cynical realism deserves a response in kind. There *is* widespread bitterness in the army; morale is low, at times mutinously so. Soldiers returning from Vietnam tell stories of men refusing direct orders and shooting officers. Drug abuse is common. Men are deserting in large numbers. The Pentagon concedes that over 98,000 men deserted in 1971 and that over 350,000 have done so since 1967, when Gillette was denied his conscientious objector classification.[41] Morale is probably as low as it has ever been. And the condition is certainly exacerbated by the presence within the army of vocal opponents of the war who express their feelings, turn out GI newspapers, and organize open resistance. The center of the antiwar movement has in fact shifted from the college campuses to military bases on the one hand, and to the federal prisons on the other. The government, so concerned about morale, must weigh the disruption that might result from the quiet deferment of conscientious war opponents against the disruption that results even now from their presence in the army or from their conspicuous imprisonment. It is a grim utility calculation indeed.

If my argument is sound, neither of the two governmental interests weighed by the Supreme Court in *Gillette* would be seriously jeopardized should conscientious objector deferments be made available to selective objectors. These interests would be no more compromised than they are under the present system. In the absence of such overriding considerations it is unconstitutional to recognize one sort of religious objection to partipation in war but not another. Guy Gillette should not have been sent to prison.

41. *New York Times*, 28 Dec. 1971, p. 9.

THE CONTRIBUTORS

R. B. BRANDT is Professor of Philosophy and Chairman of the Department of Philosophy at the University of Michigan. He is the author of *Ethical Theory* and other books on moral and political theory.

R. M. HARE is White's Professor of Moral Philosophy in the University of Oxford and Fellow of Corpus Christi College, Oxford. His writings include *The Language of Morals* and, most recently, *Essays on Philosophical Method* and *Practical Inferences and Other Essays.*

SANFORD LEVINSON, who holds a Ph.D. in Political Science from Harvard and a J.D. from Stanford Law School, has taught at Ohio State University and is currently clerking for U.S. District Judge James B. McMillan in Charlotte, North Carolina.

DAVID MALAMENT is a graduate student in the Department of Philosophy at The Rockefeller University. He was recently released from the federal prison in Danbury, Connecticut, after serving a sentence for refusing induction into the army.

THOMAS NAGEL is Professor of Philosophy at Princeton University. He has written *The Possibility of Altruism* and a number of articles on ethics and the philosophy of mind.

MICHAEL WALZER is Professor of Government at Harvard University. His books include *The Revolution of the Saints: A Study in the Origins of Radical Politics* and *Obligations: Essays on Disobedience, War, and Citizenship.* The study of war and morality now engaging his attention will be issued, on completion, in book form.

RICHARD WASSERSTROM is Professor of Law and Professor of Philosophy at U.C.L.A. He is the author of *The Judicial Decision* and editor of *War and Morality* and *Morality and the Law.*

A *Philosophy & Public Affairs* Reader

Titles available:

THE RIGHTS AND WRONGS OF ABORTION
WAR AND MORAL RESPONSIBILITY